Family Secrets

TO MY THREE CHILDREN,
NAYESHA, ROWAN & NIRAN,
KEEP COOKING, LEARNING & MOST
OF ALL ENJOY THE FOOD.

www.currycuisinecookeryschool.co.uk

Published by Prett Tejura
Photography by Sue Hiscoe
Design and Print by Digitronix, Brighouse

ISBN 978-0-9926961-0-8

Contents

FOREWORD

Prett & Paresh Tejura are an absolute tour de force and a nicely formidable combination at that. They also have shared views on food & family values.

It was inevitable they'd find their way into the food business and 6 years on, Prett's cookery school, Curry Cuisine, has proved highly successful and inspirational for those lucky enough to have attended. Their chutney, pickle and spice business reflects a lifetime's worth of knowledge inspired by the influence of previous generations.

In Prett's 'Family Secrets' we get an insight into her upbringing, much of which was spent at her mother's arm in the family kitchen in West Yorkshire, although she was born in Kenya. The big difference between Prett and her mum's kitchen, is that she allows her sons and husband to get involved and although her speciality is Indian cuisine, dishes from all over the culinary planet are now birthed in Chateau Tejura.

Not surprisingly I've learnt that pre-children Prett and Paresh tasted their way round India and the recipes in this book reflect that journey, dipping into street food en route to full on banqueting dishes, fit for the finest of weddings. Prett conjures up powerful images of whole Gujarati communities, pulling together when the merest hint of a celebration occurred.

Her 'Wedding Style Black Chickpeas' is based on early memories of Indian weddings. The fact that she calls it 'Tingy Tangy Chickpea', tells us a lot about Prett's humour. Also, from my experience of sharing a stage with her at cookery demos, you're always better doing what she tells you; it just saves time!

'Fish Masala' is the type of dish which would entice even the most piscatorially challenged to dive in. Okra, or lady's fingers, is a marvellous vegetable, but too often it turns out as a slimy mess, but Prett tells us exactly how to avoid this, and when combined with potatoes it turns into a triumph.

Prett's little tips are invaluable. 'Perfect Basmati Rice should be just wet enough to be squeezed'. She gives clear indication as to how spicy or easy or difficult the dishes are to recreate. Her enticing 'Mango and Pistachio Cheesecake' has a straightforward 2 cookery spoon rating.

Even Paresh gets a look in with his 'Chilli Paneer', an Indo/Chinese dish, inspired by trips to Wembley.

I'm encouraged to track down tindola, the cucumber style veg (also known as Gilora) now widely available in British Asian shops, as it sounds ace combined with onions.

It's typical of the Tejura's that this book is littered with pictures of the family taken in the kitchen or dining room, as this reflects what they're all about and is the impetus for their continued success. I'm not sure how Prett found the time to write this book, but am delighted she did!

NIGEL BARDEN
BBC food and drink broadcaster and chairman of the Great Taste Awards

Chilli Paneer. Recipe on page 76.

Welcome

I came to England with my family from Eldoret, Kenya when I was just 6 months old and although I grew up in West Yorkshire, my Gujarati origins are extremely important to me.

I realise and appreciate that the role of food and cooking with my mother and siblings have played an important part in my life, even as a young child. Food, for me, always evokes memories of family and home. From the comfort, familiarity and warm feelings of smells and flavours when cooking, to the use of herbs and spice combinations in a favoured dish or preparing traditional food; all of this has served to reinforce and strengthen familiar bonds. Discovering and creating new dishes as I developed friendships with people from a wide range of international backgrounds and heritage has encouraged me to embark on a journey; a journey which has enabled me to travel the world from my kitchen table.

It was my mother who inspired me to cook. Ours was a traditional (you could say typical) household. I am the fourth child of five siblings, and everyone was expected to carry out chores and help around the house. My mother was always busy in the kitchen with a view that no-one was too young to help. My earliest memories are of peeling the skin from garlic cloves and ginger and to this day I only need to smell a hint of either of these to bring a smile to my face as happy memories come flooding back. I would watch as my mother brought together a colourful array of herbs and spices, and marvel at her ability to create dishes without referring to a recipe, measuring spoon or weighing scales.

As my culinary skills developed, I was promoted to making chapattis - a traditional Indian flat bread (page 120). My sisters and I would take turns to decide who would roll the dough into flatbreads and who would cook them. This was a task never entrusted to the boys.

The kitchen was a happy place, full of laughter and stories, as well as one of structure and discipline. This provided an environment where the informal hierarchy of family and respect for tradition, culture and history could be affirmed.

This was no more apparent than when preparing celebratory meals for special occasions like weddings and religious events such as Diwali.

Preeti Tejura

1937

I would watch as my mother brought together a colourful array of herbs and spices, and marvel at her ability to seemingly create dishes without reference to a recipe, measuring spoon or weighing scales.

Often extended family and neighbours would descend on each other's kitchens, or individually prepare a dish, which formed a key component of an overall meal. This formed the backdrop for family and friends to get together, swap traditional stories and reminisce; a unique opportunity to celebrate our heritage.

As we are Gujarati, the majority of the meals I ate when younger, were vegetarian. Our East African experience, however, also encouraged us to eat meat, fish, chicken masala and lamb curry dishes which, until now, are family secrets, but you will find the recipes here in the book.

My personal favourites are probably the vegetarian dishes. Gujarati vegetarian dishes are considered to be among the world's best and Tuwar Dhal (page 42), Bombay potatoes, chapattis and rice are a Saturday lunchtime, much-loved favourite, with my family. You may have guessed from what I have said, family is very important to me. Family meals in my house are different to what I experienced, as they are a mix of traditional Indian, Italian, English, Thai and Mexican cuisine, with the occasional fusion dish.

My children now assist me in the kitchen in the same way my sisters, and I helped my mother. We are committed to using fresh ingredients, wherever possible, we cook from scratch, eat and enjoy the meal together.

For me, this keeps us close as a family, acknowledges our heritage and retains our culture, though not to the exclusion of others. The one difference between mum and I is that I allow my boys and my husband Paresh into the kitchen - so he can peel the garlic and ginger!

Seriously, Paresh and I share a passion for good food and particularly good Indian cuisine. We have had many discussions about opening our own café-deli and food business. We travelled the 'Indian Golden Triangle' between Delhi, Agra and Jaipur before the children were born, enjoying eating in cafes or the street food. With our children, we then travelled to southern India, particularly to Kerela. By spending time away from major cities our eyes opened to the range and sheer diversity of foods and cooking styles on offer and to the innovative use of ingredients. This is an experience I bring to my cookery school and my home cooking every day.

It's hard to believe now but those influences have helped Paresh and I to realise our dream and run our own business. Our small, but perfectly formed, Curry Cuisine Cookery School continues to grow since it was founded more than six years ago. We developed our own range of traditionally handcrafted spice mixes, chutneys, dessert sauces and spice inspired jams - many of which have won major awards.

Our travel experiences and teaching in my cookery school are the catalysts to me writing this book. We are, seemingly, constantly being told that 'curry' is the most popular dish in the UK; you only have to look over the supermarket shelves piled high with curry sauces and powders, spices and accompaniments. Every town centre has Indian restaurants and takeaways.

Nevertheless, so few people have tasted authentic Indian cuisine, or had the courage and know-how to try cooking the food at home. Despite the complex flavours, in reality, Indian cookery is relatively simple and most dishes can be adapted to personal taste.

This lack of cooking authentic Indian food comes from lack of familiarity with the ingredients, concern that 'it will go wrong', insufficient time, etc. With a little preparation, a willingness to experiment - plus getting the family to join in - you can create tasty authentic Indian meals for a fraction of the cost of buying the meal in.

I know many of the recipes throughout this book will soon become family favourites and be visited time and again. I hope you enjoy experimenting - remember each recipe is a guide and don't be scared to try something new!

It's hard to believe now that those influences have helped Paresh and I realise our dream to run our own business and that our small, but perfectly formed curry cuisine cookery school continues to grow since it was founded more than 6 years ago.

Spice Guide

India is a very large country, with major variations in climate, religion, local produce and customs, leading to diverse ways of preparing and serving food.

However, a common theme that runs throughout Indian cookery is the careful blending of spices in different combinations and quantities to add flavour and that unique taste. This is often referred to as garam masala, and would generally consist of a range of spices appearing or known to that area. I have included my mum's own garam masala spice blend, which is a more rounded blend suitable for most Indian dishes but especially for the gujarati dishes used everyday.

The list of spices is endless, but I have included those that are used throughout the book which give a particular flavour.

A question often asked is how long to keep and store spices. Spices must be stored in a dark place or cupboard, not on your kitchen worktop. Ensure they are kept in airtight jars and for a maximum of two years.

So it may be a good time to clear out those spice cupboards and start a fresh.

Spices

MUSTARD SEEDS

The brown ones (rai) are mainly used in Indian cooking and impart a distinctive, slightly tart flavour.

CUMIN SEEDS

They are used to add a mild, sweet aromatic flavour to curries and accompaniments such as pickles and yoghurt dishes. The crushed seeds are an important ingredient in garam masala.

CORIANDER & CUMIN POWDER

A blend of 2 parts coriander to 1 part cumin. This combination adds flavour and not heat.

CHILLI

There are a variety of chillies, the bigger they are the milder their flavour. We mainly use small green finger chillies with the seeds to add heat to the dish. Red chillies are ripened green ones and can be equally as hot.

TURMERIC

This is a plant root ground and sold in powdered form. It gives the characteristic yellow colour to Indian curries. It has many health benefits more recently has links to helping ward off dementia and reduce your risk of cancer.

GARAM MASALA

This spice mix is used in most dishes and it is generally specific to the household.

This is a peppery blend used to add heat and flavour, so season as you would black pepper.

FENUGREEK SEEDS

These flat, beige seeds can be bitter and are normally used sparingly to impart a unique flavour to dishes.

CINNAMON

This is the dried bark of the cinnamon shrub used in meat dishes but can also be found in the powdered form for puddings.

CARDAMON PODS

There are two main types used in Indian food: large brown pods and smaller green pods. Both pods are used to flavour curries and rice as well as in Garam masala. The green pods are often ground and added to sweet dishes. The brown pods have a smokey flavour.

CLOVES

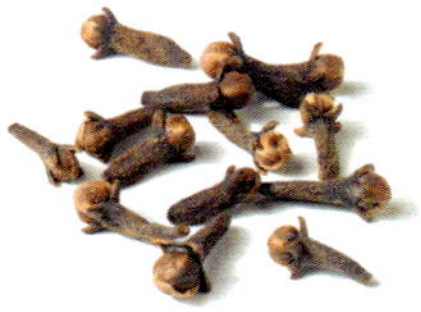

These are the dried buds of a tree native to the Spice Islands in Indonesia. Whole cloves are used in meat dishes whilst the ground ones with fruit.

CORIANDER LEAVES

Its parsley like leaf used to add flavour to the dish as well as a garnish.

CORIANDER SEEDS

These seeds are one of the defining spices of Indian food. They form the basis of most if not all curry powders.

SPICES

PAPRIKA

Derived from pimiento red peppers, it is used to impart a red colour to Indian dishes and gives a sweet flavour. It is a key ingredient within tandoori masala.

STAR ANISE

Star anise is shaped like an eight-pointed star and contains seeds with an aniseed flavour, which comes from the spice's essential oil, anethole. It is used as a spice in preparation of biryani and it is a component of garam masala.

MACE (JAVENTRY)

This is the outer casing of a nutmeg so has very similar aroma and uses. Probably a little stronger than nutmeg and is used in various spice blends, my favourite is within Rogan Josh.

FENNEL SEEDS

These are light green in colour and look similar to cumin seeds but have a distinct flavour of liquorice. It is used in a lot of Eastern dishes and also helps to aid digestion. These are the sweet mouth fresheners you often get in the Indian restaurants at the end of the meal.

AJWAIN (CAROM SEEDS)

A small, dark green seed with flavours similar to thyme. It is mainly used with hard to digest vegetables and as flavouring in breads.

JAGGERY

This is raw cane sugar with a distinctive sweet, fudgy taste, used to enrich sauces and desserts.

SAFFRON

Saffron is the dried stamens of the crocus flower. This spice is used sparingly as it is very expensive. The strands give food a yellow, orange colour and a delicate honey flavour.

TAMARIND

The pulp of the dark brown tamarind fruit pod is compressed and dried into a concentrated sticky block. It adds a sweet and sour taste to dishes and chutneys.

BAY LEAVES

A dried, flat leaf used to flavour sauces and curries.

Garam Masala

My mum's own secret recipe. This is a peppery blend used to add heat and flavour, so season as you would black pepper.

INGREDIENTS

- **1 tsp coriander seeds**
- **1 tsp cumin seeds**
- **½ tsp whole cloves**
- **½ tsp whole black pepper**
- **¼ tsp black cardamon**
- **¼ tsp star anise**
- **5cm cinnamon stick**
- **½ tsp ginger powder**
- **¼ tsp bay leaves (dried)**
- **¼ tsp fennel seeds**

HOW TO PREPARE

1. Mix all the ingredients together in a bowl.
2. Grind to a powder.
3. Store in air tight container. This will keep for 3-6 months.

Tea Masala

A subtle blend of spices, when used in tea creates the perfect cuppa. It is invigorating and relaxing all at the same time and great for those lazy Sunday mornings.

INGREDIENTS

- **1 tbsp black peppercorns**
- **1 tbsp green cardamon pods**
- **1 tsp cinnamon powder**
- **1 tsp ginger powder**

HOW TO PREPARE

1. Place all ingredients in spice grinder and blend to a fine powder. Store in an air tight jar.

HOW TO MAKE 2 MUGS

1. In a milk pan or small sauce pan add 1 mug of water and start to boil.
2. Add half a teaspoon of the tea masala, 2 tea bags or 1 tsp tea leaves and sugar if required.
3. Once it starts to boil add a mug of milk, stir.
4. Once this starts to come to the boil, turn down and simmer for a minute.
5. Strain into the mugs or tea pot.

Traditional Indian Food

To cover the basics from creating a masala sauce to creamy dhals and exotic vegetables, all with their unique spicing. Easy to follow with good flavours and accessible ingredients.

CHICKEN MASALA

Sunday dinner would not be the same without this dish. Generally used with chicken on the bone to create a saucy, tomato based curry. Our signature chicken curry and base sauce where the layering of spices is critical as well as the cooking technique.

INGREDIENTS

- **600g chicken breasts (chopped into small squares or chicken on the bone)**
- **1 medium onion finely chopped**
- **5cm stick cinnamon**
- **4 cloves**
- **2 tbsp sunflower oil**
- **1 ½ tsp crushed garlic**
- **1 tsp chopped ginger**
- **½ can chopped tomatoes**
- **1 tsp salt (to taste)**
- **2 tsp coriander & cumin powder**
- **1 tsp garam masala**
- **½ tsp turmeric powder**
- **¼ tsp red chilli powder**
- **1 tsp chopped green chillies**
- **handful fresh coriander chopped**

SERVES	SPICE	DIFFICULTY
4		

HOW TO COOK

1. Place the oil in a cooking pan and heat, add cloves and cinnamon and wait until they sizzle.
2. Add the onions and cook until they turn golden on a medium to low heat stirring occasionally. This may take up to 10 minutes.
3. Add the garlic and ginger and sauté for 1 minute to release any raw aromas.
4. Add the powdered spices and salt, stir and cook for 1 minute. Add a little water here if the paste begins to stick.
5. Add the tomatoes and green chillies.
6. Simmer for 5-10 minutes with the lid on. The masala will be ready when the oil appears on the surface.
7. Place the chicken into the pan and stir. Cook on high heat (with lid on) to sear the chicken and the masala is well mixed into the meat. Approx. 5 minutes.
8. Reduce the heat to low and cook for a further 15-20 minutes, stirring occasionally. Pour some hot water into the pan if required. (Approx. 50mls)
9. Add the fresh coriander, cook for a further 5 minutes.
10. Serve with boiled basmati rice (pg. 128) or Chapattis (pg. 120).

Chicken Makhani

One I created to cater for my children and those who are new to spice. This is a mild dish for everyone to enjoy and great for the family.

INGREDIENTS

- **600g chicken breasts**
- **1 medium onion finely chopped**
- **2 tbsp sunflower oil**
- **¼ can of chopped tomatoes**
- **1 ½ tsp salt (to taste)**
- **2 tsp coriander & cumin powder**
- **½ tsp turmeric powder**
- **¼ tsp red chilli powder**
- **1 ½ tsp crushed garlic**
- **4 fl oz double cream**
- **handful fresh coriander chopped**

SERVES **4** SPICE DIFFICULTY

HOW TO COOK

1. Place the oil in a saucepan and heat.
2. Add the onions and cook until they turn golden.
3. Add the chopped tomatoes, garlic and spices (except the fresh coriander) and stir.
4. Simmer for 5-10 minutes with the lid on. The sauce will be ready when the oil appears on the surface.
5. Place the chicken into the pan and stir. Cook for a while until the meat turns white and the sauce is well mixed into the meat.
6. Cook on a medium/low heat for 15 minutes or until chicken is cooked.
7. Add the cream and coriander and cook for a further 5 minutes.
8. Serve with basmati rice or Chapattis.

Lamb Meatball Curry

I have made this dish many times and eaten it with spaghetti. If you remove the sauce it becomes a great finger food for parties. Everyone loves spicy meatballs.

INGREDIENTS

- **500g lamb leg minced**
- **2 tsp salt**
- **2 tsp coriander & cumin powder**
- **1 ½ tsp garam masala**
- **1 tsp turmeric powder**
- **2 ½ tsp crushed garlic**
- **2 tsp chopped ginger**
- **½ tsp red chilli powder**
- **2 tsp chopped green chillies**
- **2 tsp lemon juice**
- **2 medium onions finely chopped**
- **5cm stick cinnamon**
- **6 cloves**
- **3 tbsp sunflower oil**
- **½ tin chopped tomatoes**
- **handful fresh coriander chopped**

SERVES	SPICE	DIFFICULTY
4-6		

HOW TO COOK

1. Marinate the meat. Add the following ingredients to the meat: salt, ginger, garlic, green chilli and half of the following spices; turmeric, coriander & cumin powder, garam masala and lemon juice. Mix and leave to one side.
2. Place the oil in a cooking pan and heat, add the cloves and cinnamon into the oil and wait until they sizzle.
3. Place the onions into the pan and cook until they turn golden. Stir while cooking. Add the tomatoes and stir. Add the remainder of the coriander & cumin powder, red chilli, turmeric and garam masala.
4. Make up the meatballs and place into the tomato masala. Alternatively, cook the meatballs in the oven gas mark 7 (220˚c) for 10 minutes to seal.
5. Use a small spoon to carefully stir them into the mixture. Cover and cook for 10 minutes on a medium/low heat.
6. Add some water if more sauce is required and the chopped coriander. Stir carefully and simmer with the lid on for 10 minutes.
7. Serve with chapattis, naan or even spaghetti.

Keema Curry

*This is a really quick, cheap and easy recipe.
It is one of my boys' favourite especially when
my mum makes it.*

INGREDIENTS

- 1kg lamb leg minced
- 2 tsp salt
- 2 tsp coriander & cumin powder
- 1 ½ tsp garam masala
- 1 tsp turmeric
- ½ tsp red chilli powder
- 2 ½ tsp crushed garlic
- 2 tsp chopped ginger
- 2 tsp chopped green chillies
- 2 tsp lemon juice
- 2 medium onions finely chopped
- 5cm stick cinnamon
- 6 cloves
- 3 tbsp sunflower oil
- ¼ tin chopped tomatoes
- 110g frozen peas (optional)
- 200g potato, part boiled (optional)
- handful fresh coriander chopped

SERVES	SPICE	DIFFICULTY
4-6		

HOW TO COOK

1. Marinate the meat. Add the following ingredients to the meat: salt, ginger, garlic, chilli (red and green), turmeric, coriander and cumin powder, garam masala and lemon juice. Mix and leave to one side.
2. Place the oil in a cooking pan and heat, add the cloves and cinnamon into the oil and wait until they sizzle.
3. Place the onions into the pan and cook until they turn golden. Stir while cooking.
4. Add the mince and stir to ensure the meat is separated. 4-5 minutes.
5. Put the lid on and cook for a further few minutes.
6. Add the tomatoes, chopped coriander and some water (75ml) and simmer with the lid on for 10 minutes. (Add peas and part boiled potatoes now if using).
7. Serve with chapattis, naan or even spaghetti.

GOSHT

(LAMB WITH AUBERGINES)

This is one of my favourites. Rich spicy lamb, flavoured with aubergines to create a thick sauce. Great served with Methi parata's. (see pg 124)

INGREDIENTS

- **1.25kg lamb pieces on the bone**
- **4 tbsp sunflower oil**
- **4 medium onions finely chopped**
- **10cm stick cinnamon**
- **4 cloves**
- **2 tsp salt**
- **2 tsp coriander & cumin powder**
- **1 tsp garam masala**
- **1 tsp turmeric powder**
- **1 tsp red chilli powder**
- **1 ½ tsp crushed garlic**
- **2 tsp chopped ginger**
- **1 tsp chopped green chillies**
- **1 medium aubergine finely diced**
- **400g chopped tomatoes**
- **handful fresh coriander chopped**

SERVES	SPICE	DIFFICULTY
6		

HOW TO COOK

1. Place the oil in a cooking pan and heat, place the cloves and cinnamon into the oil and wait until they sizzle.
2. Place the onions into the pan and cook until they turn golden. Stir while cooking, this may take 8–15 minutes.
3. Add the ginger and garlic to the pan and stir.
4. Add the turmeric, garam masala, red chilli powder, coriander & cumin powder and salt in the pan. Stir and cook for 1 minute.
5. Add the tin of tomatoes to the pan and the green chillies.
6. Stir and cover, let the sauce cook for 10 minutes until the oil appears around the edges.
7. Add the lamb and aubergine, stir and cook on medium heat for 10 minutes or longer.
8. Turn the heat to a simmer and cook for 30-45 minutes, until the lamb is tender, (make sure you put the lid on).
9. Chop the coriander and add to the pan.

Fish Masala

This is a family favourite on Fridays. Quick, easy and great for converting those that say they don't like fish. Uses fresh tomatoes, together with coriander and lemon to provide a clean, fresh tasting dish.

INGREDIENTS

- **400g white fish (cod, haddock etc)**
- **2 fresh tomatoes finely diced (or ⅓ tin tomatoes)**
- **1 tsp salt (to taste)**
- **1 ½ tsp coriander & cumin powder**
- **1 tsp garam masala**
- **½ tsp turmeric powder**
- **¼ tsp red chilli powder**
- **1 tsp crushed garlic**
- **1 tsp chopped green chillies**
- **2 tbsp sunflower oil**
- **1 tsp fenugreek seeds**
- **2 tsp lemon juice**
- **handfull fresh coriander chopped**

SERVES 2 | SPICE | DIFFICULTY

HOW TO COOK

1. Slice the fish into big wedges or leave whole. Place to one side.
2. In a separate bowl add all the other ingredients except the oil and lemon juice. Mix and then add the fish. Marinate for 30 minutes or longer in the fridge.
3. Put the oil in a wide based frying pan and heat. Add the fenugreek seeds and let them sizzle.
4. Add the marinated fish slowly into the pan and cook gently turning once. Slowly squash the tomatoes being careful not to break the fish.
5. Fish is cooked when it appears white and flesh like. Serve with chapattis.

PRAWN POORI

My take on the restaurant version. This is more of a sizzling dish with the prawns marinated and then stir fried. Great as a starter, served with small pooris and we often serve this at our curry club evenings.

INGREDIENTS

- **20 medium prawns**
- **2 tbsp sunflower oil**
- **¼ tsp ajwain or cumin seeds**
- **1 medium onion finely chopped**
- **1 tsp salt (to taste)**
- **1 ½ tsp coriander & cumin powder**
- **¼ tsp garam masala**
- **¼ tsp turmeric powder**
- **¼ tsp red chilli powder**
- **2 tbsp chopped red peppers**
- **1 tsp chopped ginger**
- **2 fresh chopped tomatoes**
- **1 ½ tsp lemon juice**
- **handful fresh coriander chopped**

SERVES	SPICE	DIFFICULTY
4		

HOW TO COOK

1. Put the oil in a cooking pan and heat, add the ajwain or cumin seeds and wait until they turn brown. Add the finely chopped onion and stir. Cook for 2-5 minutes until golden, stirring occasionally.
2. Add the turmeric, red chilli, coriander and cumin and garam masala and cook for another minute.
3. Add the chopped peppers and ginger and prawns and cook for 5 minutes until just cooked.
4. Stir in the tomatoes, lemon juice and salt and cook for a further 3-4 minutes.
5. Remove from the heat, add the coriander and serve on poori's (page 122).

Cauliflower, Potato & Peas Curry

This recipe is a regular feature in our homes, its simple, bold flavours shine through perfectly. It differs from its Punjabi cousin (as eaten in most restaurants) in its light and fresh taste. Great with lime pickle and chapattis.

INGREDIENTS

- **1 medium size cauliflower cut into florets.**
- **225g potatoes (peeled & diced)**
- **110g frozen peas**
- **½ tsp mustard seeds**
- **2 tsp crushed garlic**
- **1 ½ tsp chopped ginger**
- **1 tsp chopped green chillies**
- **1 tsp salt**
- **½ tsp red chilli powder**
- **½ tsp turmeric powder**
- **2 tsp coriander & cumin powder**
- **½ tsp garam masala**
- **2 fresh tomatoes (diced)**
- **handful fresh coriander chopped**

SERVES	SPICE	DIFFICULTY
4		

HOW TO COOK

1. Place the oil in a cooking pan and heat, add the mustard seeds and wait until they sizzle/pop.
2. Add the cauliflower, peas and potatoes and stir. Keep the pan on a medium heat.
3. Add the garlic, ginger and green chillies
4. Add the rest of the dried spices and stir.
5. Cook for a few minutes with the lid on and on a medium to low heat.
6. Add the fresh tomatoes, fresh coriander and stir.
7. Cover and cook on a low heat until the vegetables are cooked (approx. 15-20mins).
8. Serve with chapattis or as a side dish.

Bombay Potatoes

This dish always reminds me of the picnics we had as children. My mum would make a pan of these potatoes and a stack of chapattis for our lunch before heading off to the seaside.

INGREDIENTS

- **800g potatoes, peeled & diced into small squares (2cm)**
- **3 tbsp sunflower oil**
- **½ tsp mustard seeds**
- **½ tsp cumin seeds**
- **1 tsp salt (to taste)**
- **2 tsp coriander & cumin powder**
- **1 tsp garam masala**
- **½ tsp turmeric powder**
- **½ tsp red chilli powder**
- **1 ½ tsp crushed garlic**
- **1 tsp chopped ginger**
- **1 tsp chopped green chillies (to taste)**
- **2 tsp lemon juice**
- **handful fresh coriander chopped**

SERVES	SPICE	DIFFICULTY
4		

HOW TO COOK

1. Place the oil in a large frying pan and heat. Add the mustard and cumin seeds and wait until they sizzle/pop.
2. Add the diced potatoes and stir.
3. Add all the other ingredients and stir.
4. Cook on a medium to low heat with the lid on for 15/20 minutes or until the potatoes are cooked, stirring once. If it starts to stick add a little hot water.
5. Add the coriander and serve with chapattis or use as a filling for wraps.

TINDOLA & ONIONS

Also known as 'Gilora', a cucumber like vegetable. Often cooked with potatoes, dry and spicy with a crunch.

INGREDIENTS

- **450g Tindola (sliced)**
- **1 small onion finely chopped**
- **2 tbsp sunflower oil**
- **½ tsp mustard seeds**
- **1 tsp salt (to taste)**
- **2 tsp coriander & cumin powder**
- **½ tsp garam masala**
- **½ tsp turmeric powder**
- **¼ tsp red chilli powder**
- **1 tsp crushed garlic**
- **1 tsp chopped ginger**
- **1 tsp chopped green chillies**

SERVES	SPICE	DIFFICULTY
4		

HOW TO COOK

1. Place the oil in a cooking pan and heat, add mustard seeds and wait until they sizzle/pop.
2. Add the onions and stir until golden and soft.
3. Add all the other ingredients and stir.
4. Cook on a medium to low heat with the lid on for 10-15 minutes stirring occasionally.
5. Serve with chapattis or use as a filling for wraps.

Tuwar Dhal

This is a Saturday lunch classic dhal poured over plain boiled rice and maybe a knob of butter. My children love this dish. They like the sweet jaggery and will often run to the hob when I am tasting to give me their opinion.

INGREDIENTS

- **200g tuwar dhal**
- **2 tsp salt (to taste)**
- **½ can chopped tomatoes**
- **½ tsp turmeric powder**
- **2 tsp chopped ginger**
- **1 tsp chopped green chillies**
- **½ tsp fenugreek seeds**
- **½ tsp mustard seeds**
- **1 tbsp of sunflower oil**
- **2 tsp lemon juice**
- **3 tbsp jaggery or sugar (to taste)**
- **handful fresh coriander chopped**

SERVES	SPICE	DIFFICULTY
6	1 chilli	2 spoons

HOW TO COOK

1. Wash and soak the lentils in hot water for 1-2 hours.
2. Rinse with warm water and put onto boil, add the salt and cook until the lentils are soft and mushy.
3. Add the tomatoes, ginger, chilli and turmeric. Heat for 5 minutes. Liquidise and put to one side.
4. Place the oil in a cooking pan and heat, add the fenugreek and mustard seeds and wait until they pop.
5. Add the dhal into the oil, carefully as the mixture may splatter. Stir as the dhal heats up. Add the jaggery (or sugar), lemon juice and stir until melted.
6. Add the fresh coriander and water if the dhal is too thick. Simmer for 5 minutes.
7. Serve with boiled basmati rice or as a soup starter.

Mung Beans

Growing up this dhal was on our plates every Monday night. Simply spiced to balance and sooth the stomach after a weekend of mixed foods.

INGREDIENTS

- **200g dried green lentils (mung beans)**
- **1 tbsp sunflower oil**
- **1 ½ tsp crushed garlic**
- **1 ½ tsp chopped green chillies**
- **¼ tsp turmeric powder**
- **200g chopped tomatoes or 2 fresh tomatoes (diced)**
- **salt to taste**
- **handful fresh coriander chopped**

SERVES	SPICE	DIFFICULTY
4		

HOW TO COOK

1. Wash the lentils and add to salted water and boil. Keep adding water making sure that the beans do not boil dry.
2. Add the oil to another saucepan and heat.
3. Turn the heat down, then add the garlic and tomatoes.
4. Cover and simmer for 2 minutes
5. Add the cooked lentils, green chilli, turmeric and salt. You may need to add some water if the mixture is too thick.
6. Simmer for another 5 minutes.
7. Add the coriander and stir.
8. Serve with chapattis or rice.

Aubergine & Lilva

Aubergine's can be a bland vegetable and cooked incorrectly will put people off. In this recipe you need to ensure the aubergine is mushy for you to enjoy this curry. Lilva (broad field beans) is a creamy pea and great with aubergines. I like this dish to be spicy and it's my daughter's favourite.

INGREDIENTS

- **2 medium aubergines cut into squares**
- **300g lilva beans**
- **3 tbsp sunflower oil**
- **½ tsp ajwain (carom seeds)**
- **1 tsp crushed garlic**
- **1 tsp chopped ginger**
- **1 tsp chopped green chilli**
- **2 tsp salt**
- **¼ tsp red chilli powder**
- **½ tsp turmeric powder**
- **1 ½ tsp coriander & cumin powder**
- **½ tsp garam masala**
- **125g tin chopped tomatoes or 2 fresh tomatoes**
- **handful fresh coriander chopped**

HOW TO COOK

1. Add the oil to a cooking pan and heat, add ajwain seeds and wait until they sizzle/pop.
2. Add the aubergine and beans and stir. Keep the pan on a medium heat.
3. Add all the dried spices, garlic, ginger, green chilli and stir.
4. Cover and cook for 10 minutes on a low heat.
5. Add the tomatoes and cook for a further 30 minutes, stir occasionally.
6. If the vegetables start to stick add a little hot water.
7. Add the coriander and serve hot with chapattis.

NOTE: Don't worry if the aubergines mush up, you need to ensure the lilva beans are cooked. You should be able to squash them between your fingers.

SERVES	SPICE	DIFFICULTY
4		

Stuffed Aubergine & Potato Curry

I use the long thin aubergines here. This is a recipe I picked up when I used to cook with my mother-in-law. The main change to her recipe is the addition of garlic and ginger which she didn't use much until I came around.

INGREDIENTS

- **6 small long aubergines**
- **225g potatoes peeled & chopped into 8 pieces**
- **3 tbsp sunflower oil**
- **½ tsp mustard seeds**
- **2 tsp crushed garlic**
- **1 ½ tsp chopped ginger**
- **1 tsp chopped green chilli**
- **1 tsp salt**
- **½ tsp red chilli powder**
- **½ tsp turmeric powder**
- **2 tsp coriander & cumin powder**
- **½ tsp garam masala**
- **1 pinch sugar and lemon juice**
- **200g chopped tomatoes**
- **2 tsp lemon juice**
- **½ tsp sugar**
- **handful fresh coriander chopped**

SERVES 4 | SPICE | DIFFICULTY

HOW TO COOK

1. In a bowl mix half of the quantity of dried spices. Add the garlic, ginger, green chillies and salt with a little water to create a paste.
2. Peel the prickly top of the aubergine ensuring you leave the top intack. Cut an incision on each side deep enough to fill with spices.
3. Add some of the spice paste inside both sides of the aubergines and put to one side. Leave a little paste to coat the potatoes.
4. Take a large sauté pan and add the oil and heat. Turn the heat down and add the mustard seeds and once they start popping add the tomatoes.
5. Cook for 2 minutes stirring. Add the remainder of the dried spices, sugar, lemon and salt to season.
6. Then carefully place the aubergines and potatoes in the tomatoes and stir. Ensure the tomatoes cover and mix with the spices.
7. Cover and cook for 15-20 minutes on a medium to low heat, carefully stirring in between.
8. Check the aubergine is cooked by piercing a knife into the skin as well as the potatoes. Add the chopped coriander.
9. Serve with chapattis.

Okra & Potato

Popular Indian vegetable, cooked dry with onion and potato. Also delicious is to sprinkle with coconut before serving.

INGREDIENTS

- **450g Okra**
- **1 small onion finely chopped**
- **170g potato peeled & diced (optional)**
- **2 tbsp sunflower oil**
- **½ tsp mustard seeds**
- **1 tsp salt (to taste)**
- **2 tsp coriander & cumin powder**
- **½ tsp garam masala**
- **½ tsp turmeric powder**
- **¼ tsp red chilli powder**
- **1 tsp crushed garlic**
- **1 tsp chopped ginger**
- **1 tsp chopped green chillies (to taste)**
- **2 tsp lemon juice**

SERVES	SPICE	DIFFICULTY
2		

HOW TO COOK

1. With a damp cloth, brush and wipe the Okra. Cut into 2cm pieces.
2. Place the oil in a sauté pan and heat, add the mustard seeds and wait until they pop.
3. Add the onions and stir until golden and soft.
4. Add all the other ingredients and stir. You can also add a chopped potato here if using.
5. Cook on medium to low heat with the lid partially on for 10-15 minutes, stirring occasionally.
6. Serve with chapattis or use as a filling for wraps.

NOTE: Okra can be sticky, so try and avoid getting moisture into the vegetable. This is why the Okra is wiped clean and not washed.

Spinach & Onion Curry

This is a great way to eat spinach together with lentil rice (Kichari) and Kadi. This reminds me of our travels to India and eating at the temples. Very comforting food.

INGREDIENTS

- **600g baby leaf spinach**
- **1 medium onion finely chopped**
- **2 tbsp sunflower oil**
- **½ tsp fenugreek seeds**
- **1 tsp salt (to taste)**
- **1 ½ tsp coriander & cumin powder**
- **½ tsp garam masala**
- **¼ tsp turmeric powder**
- **½ tsp red chilli powder**
- **1 tsp crushed garlic**
- **1 tsp chopped green chillies**

SERVES	SPICE	DIFFICULTY
2		

HOW TO COOK

1. Place the oil in a large frying pan and heat. Add the fenugreek seeds and let them sizzle.
2. Then add the onions and cook until they turn golden.
3. Add the chopped spinach and spices, stir and cook for 10 minutes. Keep the lid off to allow the water to evaporate.
4. Serve with chapattis or as an accompaniment to a meal.

KADI

Yoghurt based gravy, thickened using gram flour.
Tart and spicy sauce, poured over rice or as an alternative accompaniment for those dry vegetable curries.

INGREDIENTS

- **425g natural set yoghurt**
- **1 tbsp gram flour**
- **3 curry leaves**
- **2 tsp ghee**
- **½ tsp cumin seeds**
- **1 tsp chopped garlic**
- **1 tsp chopped green chillies**
- **½ tsp salt**
- **½ tsp turmeric powder**
- **cold water**
- **handful fresh coriander chopped**

SERVES	SPICE	DIFFICULTY
6		

HOW TO COOK

1. Place the yoghurt into a large mixing bowl, add the gram flour and stir.
2. Add enough cold water to make a soup consistency and whisk.
3. Add the garlic, green chilli, turmeric, salt and chopped coriander and stir.
4. Put some ghee in a saucepan and heat. Add the cumin seeds and curry leaves. Cook until they sizzle and the seeds turn brown (not burnt).
5. Pour the yoghurt mixture into the pan and stir immediately or the mixture will split. Be careful as the mixture will splutter.
6. Continue stirring until the kadi comes to the boil and turn down. Cook for a further minute.
7. Use as a sauce on rice or as a side with vegetable curries.

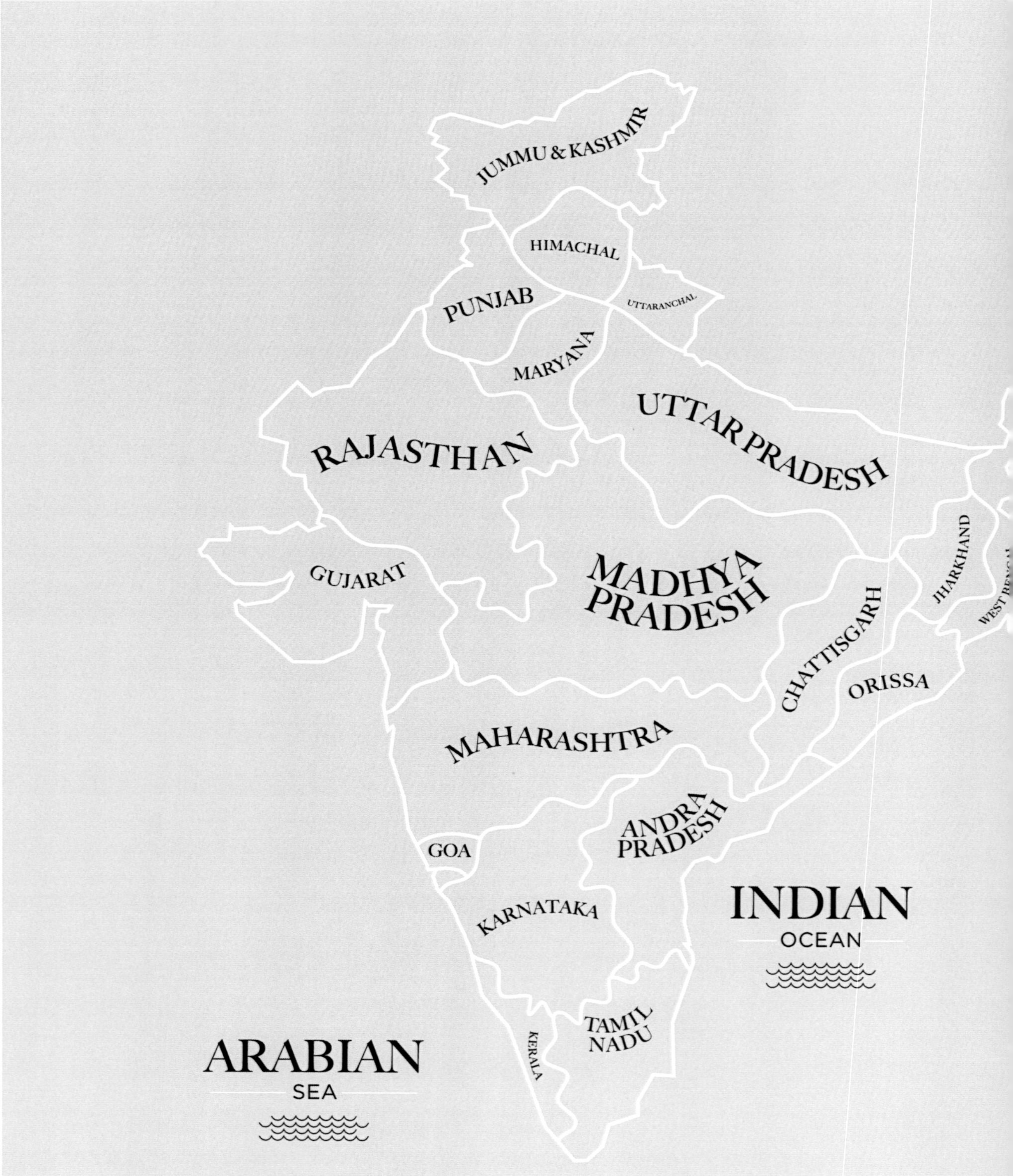
JUMMU & KASHMIR
HIMACHAL
PUNJAB
UTTARANCHAL
MARYANA
RAJASTHAN
UTTAR PRADESH
GUJARAT
MADHYA PRADESH
JHARKHAND
WEST BENGA
CHATTISGARH
ORISSA
MAHARASHTRA
ANDRA PRADESH
GOA
KARNATAKA
INDIAN
OCEAN
TAMIL NADU
KERALA
ARABIAN
SEA

Regional Map

The next few pages will give you some of my favourite regional recipes that I have picked up and discovered whilst teaching and travelling around India.

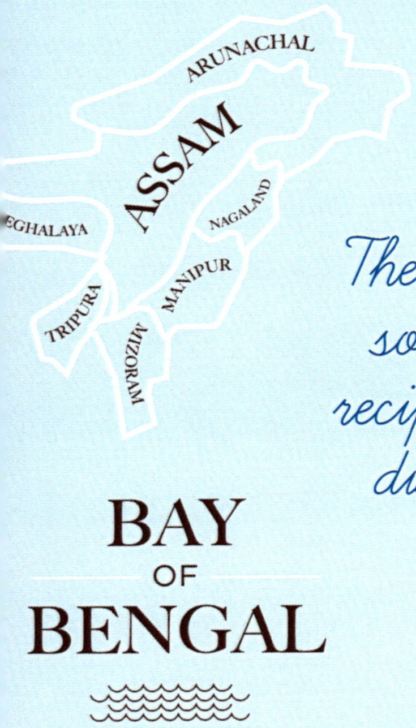

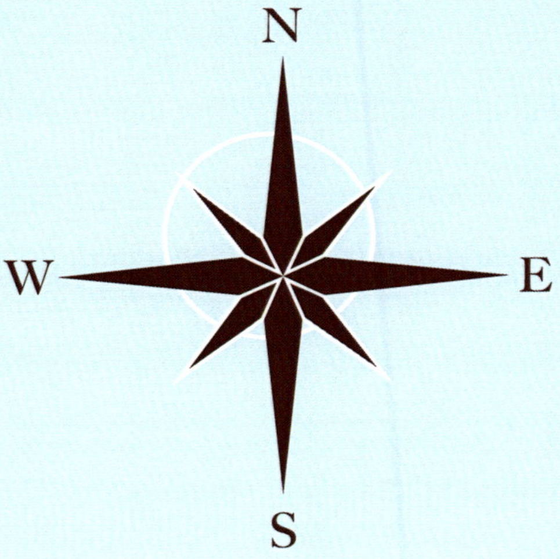

Keralan Fish

Inspired by my travels to Kerela, this dish uses the flavours of star anise, black pepper and coconut milk. Light, tasty and a great way to eat fish.

INGREDIENTS

- **500g cod/haddock loin**
- **2 tbsp sunflower oil**
- **200g shallots, chopped**
- **10 curry leaves**
- **200ml coconut milk**
- **½ tsp salt (to taste)**
- **1 tbsp lemon juice**

SPICE POWDER:

- **1 star anise**
- **2 dried red chillies**
- **1 tbsp coriander seeds**
- **½ tsp turmeric powder**
- **10 black peppercorns**
- **3 cloves**
- **3 green cardamon pods**
- **10cm stick cinnamon**

SERVES	SPICE	DIFFICULTY
4		

HOW TO COOK

1. Grind together all the ingredients for the spice powder. Set aside.
2. Add the oil into a large frying pan, karahi or wok and heat. Add the shallots and curry leaves and cook over a moderately low heat for 5 minutes until the shallots are soft.
3. Stir in the spice powder (put less in if you wish for it to be milder), salt and then add the coconut milk. Cook for 5 minutes until the sauce thickens. Stir occasionally.
4. Cut the fish into wedges and add to the sauce.
5. Pour in the lemon juice and mix carefully.
6. Cook gently for 4-5 minutes or until the fish is cooked.
7. Serve immediately with rice or mogo chips (page 94).

GOAN PORK VINDALOO

Vindaloo originates from Goa, where the cooking combines Portuguese influences with fiery Indian flavours

INGREDIENTS

- **400g pork shoulder, cut into 2.5cm cubes**
- **2 cloves**
- **2.5cm cinnamon stick**
- **1 tsp cumin seeds**
- **1 tsp coriander seeds**
- **5 black peppercorns**
- **2 green cardamon pods**
- **2-4 red chillies (to taste)**
- **3 tbsp white wine vinegar**
- **1 tsp salt (to taste)**
- **15g fresh chopped ginger**
- **20g crushed garlic**
- **5 tbsp sunflower oil**
- **1 small onion finely chopped**
- **½ tsp tomato puree**
- **3 medium chopped tomatoes**
- **handful fresh coriander chopped**

SERVES	SPICE	DIFFICULTY
4	2 chillies	2 spoons

HOW TO COOK

1. Using a spice grinder, grind the whole spices to a fine powder. Make a fine paste with the ginger, garlic, chillies and vinegar.
2. Marinate the pork along with the spices, paste and salt for a couple of hours.
3. Heat the oil in a frying pan, add the onion and cook until brown (about 8 minutes). Add the tomatoes and tomato puree and stir.
4. Next add the pork and marinade and brown gently over a moderate heat for 6-7minutes. Turn the heat to low, cover and cook until the pork is done, approx. 40 minutes.
5. Garnish with the coriander.

Bengali Chicken Curry

The cuisine of Bengal is the most influential and interesting, with a combination of Hindu and Muslim foods. Flavours of black cardamon, red chillies and Bengal garam masala, gives this dish a fiery touch.

INGREDIENTS

- **750g chicken breasts/ 1.2kg chicken joints**
- **70ml mustard oil**
- **300g onion finely chopped**
- **1 dried red chilli**
- **10cm stick cinnamon**
- **3 cloves**
- **3 black cardamon pods**
- **1 bay leaf**
- **200g chopped tomatoes**
- **1 tsp salt (to taste)**
- **1 tsp coriander powder**
- **1 tsp turmeric powder**
- **1 tsp red chilli powder**
- **1 tsp crushed garlic**
- **1 tsp chopped ginger**
- **½ tsp Bengal garam masala**

SERVES	SPICE	DIFFICULTY
4		

HOW TO COOK

1. Place the oil in a cooking pan and heat, turn to medium heat, add dried chillies, whole spices and bay leaf, sauté until they crackle.
2. Add the onions and cook until they turn golden.
3. Add the ginger and garlic and cook for 2-3 minutes.
4. Add the chicken pieces and seal on both sides.
5. Add the red chilli, coriander and turmeric powder, stir and sauté for 1 minute.
6. Stir in the chopped tomatoes, salt and 100ml of water. Bring to a simmer and cook gently for about 20 minutes until the chicken is cooked.
7. Sprinkle some Bengal garam masala and serve with steamed rice.

NOTE: Bengali garam masala uses equal quantities of cloves, cinnamon, green cardamon with a couple of bay leafs ground together.

Northern Rogan Josh

This is a dish I always choose in restaurants, so finding this recipe is great. It uses ground almonds and tomato purèe to create a sauce, with a strong intense aroma from the saffron, mace and pepper.

INGREDIENTS

- 1kg chicken joints or 600g chicken breast
- 50g natural yoghurt
- pinch saffron
- 2 tbsp crushed blanched almonds
- 2 medium onions finely sliced
- 4 tbsp sunflower oil
- 1 ½ tsp crushed garlic
- 2 tsp chopped ginger
- 1 tsp salt (to taste)
- 2 tsp coriander powder
- ½ tsp garam masala
- ½ tsp turmeric powder
- 1 tsp red chilli powder
- 2 tbsp tomato paste
- handful fresh coriander chopped

GARAM MASALA:

- 1 tsp cumin seeds
- 5 green cardamon pods
- 2 black cardamon pods
- 2cm cinnamon stick
- 6 cloves
- 2 mace blades
- 2 tsp black peppercorns

SERVES	SPICE	DIFFICULTY
4		

HOW TO COOK

1. Marinate the chicken with the yoghurt, saffron and almonds for 30 minutes.
2. Prepare the garam masala by pounding the spices together in a spice grinder or pestle and mortar.
3. Heat the oil in a pan; add the pounded garam masala mix and stir until the spices crackle. Add the sliced onions and cook for approximately. 10 minutes until softened and golden brown.
4. Add the ginger and garlic to the pan and stir for 1-2mins.
5. Add the chicken with the marinade, stir and cook for 15 minutes until the meat is browned. Keep stirring scraping the bottom of the pan. You may wish to add a little water or chicken stock if it is really dry.
6. Add the other powdered spices and cook for 3-5 minutes, adding water if required.
7. Stir in the salt and tomato paste and cook until the chicken is tender.
8. Chop the coriander and add to the pan.
9. Serve with rice or chapattis.

Chettinad Kofta Curry

(Tamil Nadu, South India)

This is a spicy curry using sliced onions creating a different texture, which I like. The fennel and black pepper give a distinctive flavour to this dish. Also great with cauliflower, potatoes or chickpeas.

INGREDIENTS

- **500g lamb leg minced**
- **70ml sunflower oil**
- **200g onions (sliced)**
- **20 curry leaves**
- **2 tsp red chilli powder**
- **2 tsp coriander powder**
- **2 tsp turmeric powder**
- **400ml coconut milk**
- **½ tsp salt (to taste)**
- **100g chopped tomatoes**
- **2 tbsp chopped coriander**

SPICE PASTE:

- **1 tbsp chopped ginger**
- **2 tbsp crushed garlic**
- **3 cloves**
- **10 black peppercorns**
- **1 ½ tsp fennel seeds**
- **2.5cm stick cinnamon**

SERVES	SPICE	DIFFICULTY
4		

HOW TO COOK

1. Make the spice paste in a blender with 3 tbsp water into a fine paste.
2. Heat 50ml of sunflower oil in a deep sauté pan, add the onions and cook until softened and light brown.
3. Add the curry leaves and spice paste and cook for 2-3 minutes, then add half the ground spices and cook for another 30 seconds.
4. Add the coconut milk, salt and tomatoes. Bring to a simmer and cook for 20 minutes.
5. In a bowl season the minced lamb with 1 tsp of salt and the remainder of the ground spices.
6. Roll into small balls. Add 20ml of sunflower oil into a frying pan and gently fry the meatballs for 2-3 minutes until brown.
7. Add the meatballs to the sauce and simmer for 10-15 minutes with the lid off.
8. Sprinkle with chopped coriander before serving.

CABBAGE THORAN

This recipe was picked up during my Keralan home stay. Many of the vegetable dishes are called thoran as they are stir fried with coconut, mustard seeds and curry leaves for their unique flavour. Great as a warmed cabbage salad.

INGREDIENTS

- **500g cabbage (finely shredded)**
- **200g carrots (grated)**
- **3 tbsp sunflower oil**
- **½ tsp mustard seeds**
- **5 curry leaves**
- **½ tsp kalunji seeds**
- **½ tsp turmeric powder**
- **1 tsp chopped green chillies**
- **50g grated coconut**
- **½ tsp salt (to taste)**

SERVES **4** SPICE DIFFICULTY

HOW TO PREPARE

1. Place the oil in a cooking pan and heat, add the mustard seeds and when they start popping add the kalunji seeds, curry leaves and chillies and sauté for a while.
2. Add the coconut and stir.
3. Add all the other ingredients and stir. Cook for 5 minutes until soft but still with a bite.
4. Serve as an accompaniment or on its own.

Street Food & Nibbles

The all time favourite snacks to eat with a drink or with a cup of Indian tea.

GOKULAM CANTEEN

ONION BHAJI

A popular starter or snack though not a dish we would cook everyday; we reserved the bhajis for parties and special occasions. This is a classic spiced batter that can be used to coat many different vegetables.

INGREDIENTS

- **175g Gram flour (chick pea flour)**
- **1 tbsp lemon juice**
- **2 tbsp natural yoghurt**
- **2 tsp sugar**
- **250ml luke warm water**
- **1 tsp coriander & cumin powder**
- **1 tsp garam masala**
- **½ tsp turmeric powder**
- **¼ tsp red chilli powder**
- **2 tsp chopped ginger**
- **2 tsp chopped green chillies**
- **2 tsp salt (to taste)**
- **100g grated potato (optional)**
- **1 large onion finely chopped**
- **½ tsp bicarbonate of soda or ENO (fruit salts)**
- **sunflower oil for frying**

SERVES	SPICE	DIFFICULTY
4		

HOW TO COOK

1. Mix all the ingredients excluding bicarbonate of soda, onions, oil and potato together in a bowl.
2. Add the luke warm water to form a batter. Fairly thick consistency. Leave to one side for 15 minutes for the flavours to combine.
3. Heat up the oil in a frying pan, wok or deep fat fryer.
4. Just before frying add the ENO or bicarbonate of soda into the mixture. Add 1 tsp of hot oil to the batter to activate and mix.
5. Add the chopped onions and grated potatoes.
6. Drop medium sized balls into the fryer and cook turning once for 2-4 minutes.
7. Drain and serve with mint sauce or any chutney/salsa.

NOTE: These can be cooked in advance and just reheated in an oven for 5 minutes.

Pau Bhaji

This is my older son's favourite, but it has to be hot and with buttery paus (toasted bread buns). This is a great snack to have in the cafés in India.

INGREDIENTS

- 2 tbsp sunflower oil
- 150g potato peeled & diced
- 250g frozen mixed vegetables
- 1 medium onion finely chopped
- ½ red or green pepper finely chopped
- 1 ½ tsp crushed garlic
- 1 tsp chopped ginger
- 1 tsp chopped green chilli
- 1 tsp salt (to taste)
- ½ tsp red chilli powder
- ½ tsp turmeric powder
- 1 tsp coriander & cumin powder
- 2 tbsp Pau bhaji masala
- 2 fresh tomatoes (diced) or 125g chopped tomatos
- 4 soft white bread rolls
- 1 small red onion finely diced
- handful fresh coriander chopped

SERVES	SPICE	DIFFICULTY
4		

HOW TO COOK

1. Place the oil in a saucepan and fry the onion until golden (about 8 minutes).
2. Add the vegetables, garlic, ginger and chilli and cook for 1 minute.
3. Add the rest of the dried spices, seasonings and tomatoes and stir. Add some water to allow the vegetables to cook as the mixture should be thick but mushy. Cook for 10-15 minutes or so, on a medium to low heat, until the vegetables are soft.
4. Add the fresh coriander and cook for a further 2 minutes.
5. Halve the rolls and lightly toast. Spread with butter and spoon the vegetables over, garnish with finely chopped red onion and coriander.

NOTE: You can add more butter at point 4 if you want a richer, creamier mixture.

Tandoori Chicken Wings

Marinated chicken wings, great cooked in the oven or perfect for a barbeque.

INGREDIENTS

- **10 skinless chicken wings**
- **1-2 tsp salt (to taste)**
- **2 tsp coriander & cumin powder**
- **1 tsp garam masala**
- **½ tsp turmeric powder**
- **2 tsp crushed garlic**
- **1 tsp chopped ginger**
- **2 tsp chopped green chillies**
- **2 tbsp tandoori masala**
- **100g natural yoghurt**
- **handful fresh coriander chopped**

SERVES	SPICE	DIFFICULTY
4		

HOW TO COOK

1. Place all the ingredients in a bowl and mix. Leave overnight or 30 minutes if you have time.
2. Cover an ovenproof dish with tin foil and place the chicken wings in it.
3. Cook in the middle of the oven, gas mark 7 / 220°C for 15-20 minutes, turning once.
4. Serve as a starter with mint sauce and salad.

Channa Chaat

This is a great snack which is more of an assembly than actual cooking. The ingredients are coated with a yoghurt and tamarind sauce then topped with crushed sev. Very cooling, sweet and spicy.

INGREDIENTS

- **400g black chickpeas (kala chana) flash boiled**
- **200g potato (peeled, boiled and cut into cubes)**
- **1 small red onion (diced)**
- **1 tbsp chaat masala**
- **50g sev (page 88)**
- **50ml low fat yoghurt thinned with 2 tbsp water**
- **1 tsp cumin powder**
- **½ tsp red chilli powder**
- **salt to season**
- **2 tbsp tamarind chutney (page 138)**
- **handful fresh coriander chopped**

HOW TO COOK

1. Make a base with the chickpeas and potatoes.
2. Scatter over the onions.
3. Season the yoghurt with the chaat masala and salt and drizzle over the onions and chickpeas.
4. Add the sev and tamarind chutney.
5. Sprinkle the cumin and red chilli powder.
6. Top with the coriander and eat immediately.

SERVES	SPICE	DIFFICULTY
4		

CHILLI PANEER
(INDO-CHINESE STYLE)

My husband's recipe and a cross between Indian and Chinese flavours. This dish always reminds me of our visits to Wembley, London, and eating this for lunch with crispy potato bhajis.

INGREDIENTS

- **1 tsp cornflour**
- **pinch salt**
- **1 tsp plain flour**
- **225g Paneer cut into 2cm cubes**
- **3 tbsp sunflower oil**
- **2 whole green chillies, sliced**
- **2 tsp crushed garlic**
- **1 tsp white or demerera sugar**
- **¼ tsp ground black pepper**
- **1 tbsp malt vinegar**
- **1 tbsp tomato ketchup**
- **1 tbsp dark soy sauce**
- **1 tbsp hot chilli sauce**
- **1 medium onion (finely sliced into rings)**

SERVES	SPICE	DIFFICULTY
4	2 chillies	2 spoons

HOW TO COOK

1. Mix together the cornflour, salt and flour with 1 tbsp cold water to make a thin paste.
2. Coat the paneer with the paste.
3. Heat the oil in a frying pan and lightly fry the paneer cubes for 5 minutes until golden.
4. Remove with a slotted spoon.
5. Drain on kitchen paper and set aside.
6. In the same frying pan on a low heat, gently fry the chillies, garlic, sugar, black pepper, vinegar, tomato ketchup, soy and chilli sauce with 2 tbsp boiling water for a couple of minutes.
7. Add the Paneer and mix well, smothering the Paneer cubes with the sauce. Add the sliced onions. Cook for 2-3 minutes.
8. Serve hot.

BATATA WADA
(MASHED POTATO BHAJIS)

I love this snack, especially as I love potatoes. Spicy mash rolled in a ball, dipped into batter and fried. You can also add chopped onions to the mash as an alternative.

INGREDIENTS

FOR THE MASH:

- **450g red skinned potato**
- **1 tsp chopped ginger**
- **1 tsp chopped green chillies**
- **1 tsp coriander & cumin powder**
- **¼ tsp turmeric powder**
- **¼ tsp red chilli powder**
- **1 tsp sugar**
- **2 tsp lemon juice**
- **salt to taste**
- **handful fresh coriander chopped**

WAGAR (OIL & SEEDS MIX):

- **2 tbsp sunflower oil**
- **½ tsp mustard seeds**
- **½ tsp sesame seeds**

BATTER MIX:

- **100g gram flour**
- **1 tsp red chilli powder**
- **½ tsp turmeric powder**
- **pinch salt**
- **¼ tsp ENO/bicarbonate soda**

SERVES	SPICE	DIFFICULTY
4		

HOW TO PREPARE

1. Prepare the potatoes, by peeling and boiling. Then drain and rinse with cold water. Mash and put to one side to cool.
2. Add the spices, lemon juice, sugar, chillies, coriander and salt to the mash and mix.
3. Heat the oil for the wagar and add the seeds. Once popped add to the potatoes and stir. Make into round balls (1 ½ inch in diameter).
4. Mix the ingredients for the batter, to a medium consistency, thick enough to coat the balls of potato.
5. Heat some oil in a pan or fryer, once hot enough (batter should rise to the surface), dip the potato balls into the batter and drop gently into the oil.
6. Cook for 1-2 minutes and drain on kitchen paper.
7. Serve warm with mint sauce or other dips as a starter or snack.

HANDVO

(SAVOURY SEMOLINA CAKE)

My husband's mother would always make this when she came to stay. It is great with a cup of masala tea or as a snack for breakfast.

INGREDIENTS

- **600g thick semolina powder**
- **2 medium courgettes (grated)**
- **2 medium carrots (grated)**
- **2 ½ tsp chopped ginger**
- **2 tsp crushed garlic**
- **1 ¼ tsp chopped green chillies**
- **2 ¼ tsp salt (to taste)**
- **½ tsp turmeric powder**
- **1 tsp red chilli powder**
- **handful fresh coriander chopped**
- **1 kg natural yoghurt**
- **2 tbsp eno (bicarbonate powder)**

WAGAR (OIL & SEEDS TOPPING):

- **5 tbsp sunflower oil**
- **2 tsp mustard seeds**
- **1 tsp cumin seeds**
- **3 tbsp sesame seeds**
- **5 curry leaves**

SERVES	SPICE	DIFFICULTY
6	2	3

HOW TO COOK

1. Mix all the ingredients together except ENO, yoghurt and wagar.
2. Grease an oven proof dish. Heat a small saucepan and add all the wagar ingredients, but half of the sesame seeds. Wait until the seeds pop and sizzle.
3. Place into the oven proof dish.
4. Mix the yoghurt into the dry mixture, add 2 tbsp. ENO and mix to a medium texture, like a thick batter.
5. Pour into the oven proof dish or baking tray. Sprinkle the remaining sesame seeds on top and bake in the oven, gas 6/7 (210°C) for approx. 75-80 minutes until the top is brown and the sponge cooked.
6. Serve as a snack or can be eaten for breakfast.

PAPRI
(CRISPY PASTRY DISCS)

These are the crispy discs used in the famous street food chaats.

INGREDIENTS

- **100g plain flour**
- **½ tsp salt**
- **½ tsp ground cumin powder**
- **1 tbsp sunflower oil**
- **6 tbsp water**
- **sunflower oil for deep frying**

MAKES: **50** SMALL DISCS

SPICE

DIFFICULTY

HOW TO PREPARE

1. Put the flour, salt and cumin powder into a bowl and rub in the oil. Add most of the water and mix with your hands until the mixture binds.
2. Knead firmly for 5 minutes until you have a stiff dough. Allow to rest for 15 minutes.
3. Take walnut sized pieces of the dough, roll out to a thickness of 1-2mm. Add flour to the surface if the dough starts to stick.
4. Prick the sheet all over with a fork. Using a 5cm round cutter, stamp out as many rounds as possible. Lift away the dough from around the discs, lift up the discs slowly and set aside.
5. Repeat until all the dough is used.
6. Heat the oil in a large pan/wok to a moderate temperature. Deep fry the discs, about 2-3 minutes turning once. Drain on kitchen paper and leave to cool.
7. Store in an airtight container for up to a week.

Spicy Lamb Chops

My version of the restaurant starter. Spicy marinade with yoghurt to help tenderise the lamb.

INGREDIENTS

- **12 lamb chops**
- **4 tbsp sunflower oil**
- **3 tbsp natural yoghurt**
- **1 tsp salt (to taste)**
- **2 tsp coriander & cumin powder**
- **1 tsp garam masala**
- **½ tsp turmeric powder**
- **½ tsp of red chilli powder**
- **2 tsp crushed garlic**
- **1 tsp chopped ginger**
- **1 tsp chopped green chillies**
- **2 tsp lemon juice**
- **handful fresh coriander chopped**

SERVES 6 | SPICE | DIFFICULTY

HOW TO COOK

1. Trim the chops and excess fat and put into a large bowl.
2. In a separate bowl add all the other ingredients except the oil. Mix and then add the chops.
3. Marinate overnight or for at least 2 hours.
4. Put the oil in a frying pan and heat. Fry the chops in batches for a couple of minutes on each side and then place on an ovenproof tray.
5. Cook in the oven at 200°C/gas 6 for 10 to 20 minutes depending on how pink you like your lamb.
6. Serve with an Indian side salad or mint chutney.

CHEVDO

Chevdo is a gujarati snack made usually at celebrations like Diwali. There are lots of variations of chevdo and Kenyan chevdo has it's own unique taste. I can always remember my mum preparing the ingredients and helping her make it before the festival.

INGREDIENTS

- **250g chana dhal (split chick peas)**
- **200ml full fat milk**
- **2kg red skinned potatoes**
- **500g pawa (flattened rice)**
- **100g peanuts**
- **100g whole almonds**
- **100g cashew nuts**
- **4 green chillies sliced**
- **20g dried sultanas**
- **¼ bunch fresh coriander**
- **5 tbsp granulated sugar**
- **2 tbsp poppy seeds**
- **2 tbsp fennel seeds**
- **2 tbsp red chilli powder**
- **2 tbsp salt**
- **1 ½ tbsp turmeric powder**
- **20 curry leaves**
- **sunflower oil for frying (approx. 2-3 litres)**

WAGAR:

- **3 tbsp sunflower oil**
- **2 tbsp sesame seeds**
- **2 tbsp mustard seeds**

MAKES	SPICE	DIFFICULTY
30 SNACK BAGS		

HOW TO COOK

PREPARATION IN ADVANCE

1. Soak the chana dhal overnight in luck warm water mixed with a cup of milk.
2. Drain and dry the chana dhal. Cover with a tea towel.
3. Wash and grate the potatoes and spread out onto another tea towel to absorb any moisture.
4. Sieve the pawa and put into a bowl.
5. Put 1 litre of oil in a big fryer and heat until the temperature reaches 180°C.
6. Deep fry the dried chana in batches. It will rest at the bottom of the pan, once it comes to the surface it is done.
7. Remove with a slotted spoon. Put the fried chana dhal onto a surface that is covered with some brown paper.

NOTE: This will need to be on a large surface area as each ingredient is piled on top as they are cooked.

We also used to pick out the nuts or make sure we had plenty in our bowl. This was one recipe I wanted to include as people seem to buy it ready made, but it is never as nice as the home cooked version. You can alter the spice level to suit tastes.

8. Next fry the grated potatoes in batches, until they are golden and crisp. Add to the dhal.
9. Check to see if there is enough oil in the fryer, if not add some more. Deep fry the pawa, you will need to be quick here as they do not take very long and will expand, so only add a small bowl at a time.
10. Next fry the peanuts, cashews and almonds in turn for about 30 seconds. Add to the pile of potatoes.
11. Then fry the green chillies, coriander and curry leaves in turn and add to the pile.
12. To the fried mix, add the spices and sugar. Mix thoroughly to ensure all flavours are equally spread over the mixture. Taste to see if you need more sugar or salt to your taste or even red chilli powder. Ensure this is done when it is warm otherwise the spices will not take to the fried mixture.
13. In a small saucepan, add the wagar ingredients. Wait until the seeds pop and pour over the mix. Again mix the ingredients.
14. Store in a bag within an airtight container or portion out into about 30 bags. Ensure you leave to cool before placing the lid on.

Sev & Gantha

Chickpea savoury noodles, our version of crisps. These can be mild or spicy and are also used to give a crunch to lots of Indian street foods like bhel and chaats.

INGREDIENTS

- **350g gram flour (chickpea flour)**
- **sunflower oil for deep frying**
- **¾ tsp of red chilli powder**
- **½ tsp turmeric powder**
- **1 ½ tsp salt**
- **150ml lukewarm water**
- **sev maker**

SERVES **10+** | SPICE | DIFFICULTY

HOW TO COOK

1. Mix all the dried ingredients together in a bowl.
2. Gradually add the water to create a soft dough.
3. Heat the oil for deep frying. (180°C) or test with a small amount of dough when dropped in the oil comes to the surface.
4. Put some of the dough into the sev maker. The one with small holes will make sev and bigger holes for ganthia.
5. Put the lid on and gradually turn the handle over the fryer. Noodle strings will fall into the fryer and continue until you have a circle. Reverse the handle to break off.
6. Fry until golden, 3-4 minutes turning once.
7. Remove with a slotted spoon onto kitchen paper.
8. Once cool, crush and store in an airtight container.
9. Eat on its own as a snack, or sprinkle over chaats for a crunchy topping.

Gantha

Sev

Vegetable Samosa

My mum's vegetable samosas, the best, but I am biased. The filling is key and whether you use ready made pastry sheets or make your own you won't be disappointed.

INGREDIENTS

- **450g frozen mixed vegetables**
- **150g onion finely chopped**
- **200g potato finely diced**
- **1 tsp cumin seeds**
- **½ tsp mustard seeds**
- **2 tbsp of sunflower oil**
- **1 tsp salt**
- **2 tsp coriander & cumin powder**
- **½ tsp garam masala**
- **½ tsp turmeric powder**
- **½ tsp red chilli powder**
- **1 tsp crushed garlic**
- **1 tsp chopped ginger**
- **1 tsp chopped green chillies**
- **2 tsp lemon juice**
- **1 tsp sugar**
- **sunflower oil for frying**

MAKES	SPICE	DIFFICULTY
20	2	3

HOW TO COOK

1. Place the oil in a cooking pan and heat, add the mustard and cumin seeds and wait until they pop and turn brown.
2. Add the onions and cook until they turn golden. Add the mixed vegetables and diced potatoes and stir.
3. Add all the other ingredients and stir. Cover and cook for approximately 10-15 minutes. Stir occasionally.
4. Set aside to cool.
5. The pastry cases of the samosas is made as follows or using the recipe (page 134).
6. Make some chapatti dough (page 120).
7. Halve the chapatti. Take one half and with the straight edge near you, fold the left side 2/3rds over the centre. Brush the top of the folded piece with some paste (flour & water), and fold the other side over it to form a cone. Press together with your fingers to seal. See page 134 for pictures.
8. Fill with the vegetable mixture. Brush the inner edges with the paste and press the top firmly together. Repeat until all the chapatti halves and filling has been used.
9. Heat the oil in a fryer until hot and shallow fry the samosas, turning frequently, until crispy and golden brown.

Jelebi

Mine and my daughter's favourite Indian dessert.

INGREDIENTS

- **250g granulated sugar**
- **250ml water**
- **150g self raising flour**
- **2 tbsp ghee**
- **½ tsp citric acid**
- **¼ tsp orange food colouring**
- **sunflower oil for deep frying**
- **squeezy sauce bottle**

HOW TO PREPARE

1. Make the syrup, first by boiling the water and sugar until the sugar is dissolved. Then simmer for 10-15 minutes until it gets sticky. Careful not to over cook as the sugar will crystallise. Leave to one side to cool.
2. In a bowl mix the flour, citric acid and food colouring. Then add some water to create a medium thick batter. Leave to stand for 10 minutes.
3. Add the ghee and mix. Put into a squeezy sauce bottle.
4. Heat the oil in a karahi or deep frying pan, 180°C, squeeze the bottle to create spirals in the oil. Cook for approximately 1 minute and remove onto kitchen paper. Continue until the batter is finished.
5. Dip the spirals into the cooled syrup.
6. Serve on the side with coconut ice cream (page 111) or on its own.

SERVES	DIFFICULTY
4	3 spoons

Mogo Chips

Also known as cassava, it resembles potato. A crispy and tasty Indian appetiser served with a hot chilli sauce or on the side with any mains.

INGREDIENTS

- **500g frozen mogo pieces**
- **1 tsp salt (to taste)**
- **sunflower oil for deep frying**

SERVES 4   DIFFICULTY

HOW TO PREPARE

1. Boil the frozen mogo in a large saucepan until just soft.
2. Drain and run cool water over them. Cut into chips, taking out the middle stem.
3. Heat the oil in the fryer.
4. Slowly fry the mogo pieces until golden and soft.
5. Drain onto kitchen paper and serve as an accompaniment.

Celebration Dishes

Here you have a mix of old and new recipes, ideal to wow anyone, and perfect for a special occassion.

Diwali Dry Fish

Diwali is not the same without some spiced fish in our house.

INGREDIENTS

- **450g white fish (cod, haddock etc)**
- **2 tbsp of sunflower oil**
- **1 tsp salt (to taste)**
- **1 ½ tsp coriander & cumin powder**
- **1 tsp garam masala**
- **½ tsp turmeric powder**
- **¼ tsp red chilli powder**
- **1 tsp crushed garlic**
- **1 tsp chopped green chillies**
- **2 tsp lemon juice**
- **handful fresh coriander chopped**

SERVES | SPICE | DIFFICULTY

2-3

HOW TO COOK

1. Slice the fish into big wedges or leave whole. Place to one side.
2. In a separate bowl add all the other ingredients except the oil. Mix and then add the fish. Marinate for 30 minutes or longer in the fridge.
3. Put the oil in a cooking pan and heat. Add the marinated fish slowly into the pan and cook gently turning once. Fish is cooked when it appears white and flesh like.
4. Serve with an Indian side salad.

Roast Chicken

This is our alternative Sunday dinner if we didn't feel like making our normal saucy chicken curry. It is served with spicy roast potatoes and vegetables.

INGREDIENTS

- **1 whole chicken, skinned and chopped into pieces**
- **1 tsp salt**
- **1 ½ tsp coriander & cumin powder**
- **1 tsp garam masala**
- **½ tsp turmeric powder**
- **½ tsp red chilli powder**
- **1 ½ tsp crushed garlic**
- **1 tsp chopped ginger**
- **¾ tsp chopped green chillies**
- **handful fresh coriander chopped**
- **3 tbsp sunflower oil**

HOW TO COOK

1. Place all the ingredients except the chicken in a bowl and mix. Add the chicken and leave overnight or for 30 minutes if you have time.
2. Cover an ovenproof dish with tin foil and place the chicken in it.
3. Cook in the middle of the oven, gas mark 6 / 200°C for 20-30 minutes, turning once.

SERVES	SPICE	DIFFICULTY
4		

Roasted Leg of Lamb with Spices

I first made this for my customers at a celebration event, the lamb was soft and had a great spicy gravy.

INGREDIENTS

- **2 kg lamb leg on the bone**
- **4 tbsp sunflower oil**
- **4 tbsp natural yoghurt**
- **2 tsp salt (to taste)**
- **3 tsp coriander & cumin powder**
- **2 tsp garam masala**
- **1 tsp turmeric powder**
- **1 tsp red chilli powder**
- **3 tsp crushed garlic**
- **2 tsp chopped ginger**
- **2 tsp chopped green chillies**
- **3 tsp lemon juice**
- **handful fresh coriander chopped**

SERVES	SPICE	DIFFICULTY
6		

HOW TO COOK

1. In a separate bowl add all the spices, yoghurt, garlic, ginger, green chillies, lemon juice and oil and mix to create a marinade.
2. In an oven proof dish, place the lamb on a wire rack. With a sharp knife, make deep cuts in the lamb.
3. Cover the leg of lamb with the marinade, getting the spices deep into the cuts. Cover with cling film.
4. Marinate overnight or for at least 2 hours.
5. Ensure the lamb comes to room temperature. Cover with foil and cook in the oven at gas mark 4 / 180°C for 1hr 30 minutes.
6. Uncover, bake for a further 30 minutes for medium or until cooked to your liking.
7. Remove from the oven. Loosely cover and let the meat rest for 30 minutes before serving.
8. Serve on a bed of kashmir saffron rice (page 132) or just slice and serve with raita.

TIP: Use the juices to create a spicy gravy.

MATTER PANEER

Paneer was always a dish we would order in a restaurant as mum never cooked it. This is like the restaurant versions you get.

INGREDIENTS

- **200g paneer - chopped into small squares**
- **1 medium onion finely chopped**
- **50g frozen or fresh peas**
- **3 tbsp sunflower oil**
- **1 tsp crushed garlic**
- **1 tsp chopped green chillies**
- **½ tsp mustard seeds**
- **½ tsp cumin seeds**
- **½ can of chopped tomatoes**
- **1 tsp salt (to taste)**
- **2 tsp coriander & cumin powder**
- **½ tsp garam masala**
- **¼ tsp turmeric powder**
- **¼ tsp red chilli powder**
- **handful fresh coriander chopped**

SERVES	SPICE	DIFFICULTY
4		

HOW TO COOK

1. Place 2 tbsp of oil in a cooking pan and heat, add cumin and mustard seeds and wait until they sizzle and pop.
2. Add the onions and cook until they turn golden, on a medium to low heat, stirring occasionally.
3. Add the garlic and chillies and sauté for 30 seconds to release any raw aromas.
4. Add the powdered spices and cook for 1 minute. Add a little water here if the paste begins to stick.
5. Add the tomatoes and a little water to create a sauce.
6. Simmer for 5-10 minutes with the lid on. The sauce will be ready when the oil appears on the surface.
7. In another frying pan add the remaining oil and gently brown the paneer for 2-3 minutes and leave to one side.
8. Add the peas to the sauce and cook on for approximately 5 minutes.
9. Add the browned paneer to the dish and stir. Add the coriander and cook for 5 minutes on a low heat.
10. Serve with boiled basmati rice or chapattis.

Vegetable Biryani

This recipe has been influenced by my mother-in-law. Her biryani is made on special occasions and we would eat it with kadi or just plain yoghurt. The fried cashew nuts were always fought after.

INGREDIENTS

MIXED VEG CURRY:

- **500g of frozen mixed vegetables**
- **1 medium onion finely chopped**
- **2 tbsp sunflower oil**
- **400g chopped tomatoes**
- **1 tsp salt (to taste)**
- **2 tsp coriander & cumin powder**
- **1 tsp garam masala**
- **½ tsp turmeric powder**
- **½ tsp red chilli powder**
- **1 tsp crushed garlic**
- **1 tsp chopped ginger**
- **½ tsp chopped green chillies**
- **handful fresh coriander chopped**

OTHER ITEMS (FOR LAYERING):

- **200g potato, peeled, diced and fried**
- **1 red onion sliced and fried**
- **50g sultanas fried**
- **100g cashew nuts fried**
- **350g uncooked basmati rice**
- **3 cloves**

SERVES	SPICE	DIFFICULTY
6	2	3

HOW TO COOK

1. Cook the rice as per boiled rice recipe (page 128), add a few cloves to the water during boiling.
2. Place the oil in a cooking pan and heat, add the onions and cook until they turn golden.
3. Add the frozen vegetables and stir.
4. Add the spices, garlic, ginger and chillies, stir and cook on a medium heat.
5. Next add the tomatoes and simmer for 5-10 minutes with the lid on.
6. Pour some hot water into the pan, just enough to cover the vegetables to create some sauce. Cook until the vegetables are soft.
7. Then add the fresh coriander stir and leave to cool.
8. Fry all the other items in turn in a deep fat fryer/karahi.
9. Take an ovenproof dish and start layering the curry, rice and fried potatoes, nuts, sultanas and onions in that order leaving some rice and fried onions for the top.
10. Sprinkle some chopped coriander on the top.
11. Bake covered in the oven for 30 minutes on gas mark 7 / 220°C.
12. Serve with raita (page 138) or kadi (page 52).

Hyderabad Dum Biryani

I collected this recipe from a hotel in Bangalore. I loved the freshness and earthiness of the flavours in the marinade. Very different to the homestyle meat biryanis I am used to.

INGREDIENTS

- **500g chicken breast, diced**
- **500g basmati rice (washed and soaked in water)**
- **2 medium onions thinly sliced**
- **5 green cardamons**
- **6 sticks cinnamon (5cm each)**
- **6 cloves**
- **2 star anise**
- **4 mace**
- **10 peppercorns**
- **1 tsp fennel seeds**
- **3 bay leaf**
- **250ml natural yoghurt**
- **2 tsp red chilli powder**
- **½ tsp turmeric powder**
- **2 tsp chopped ginger**
- **2 tsp crushed garlic**
- **1 bunch coriander leaves chopped**
- **1 bunch mint leaves chopped**
- **3 tbsp lemon juice**
- **60ml ghee/oil**
- **saffron strands dissolved in warm milk**

SERVES	SPICE	DIFFICULTY
6		

HOW TO COOK

1. Dry roast 3 cardamons, 1 cinnamon stick, 3 cloves, 1 star anise, mace, peppercorns, fennel, bay leaf and powder them.
2. In a bowl, marinate the meat with yoghurt, turmeric powder, ginger garlic paste, red chilli powder, ground masala powder, lemon juice, half of the chopped mint, coriander and salt.
3. Fry the sliced onions till brown and crisp, crush and add half of the fried onion into the meat mixture and let it marinate for 2-3 hours.
4. In boiling water add the remaining spices and cook the rice until ¾ done. Drain and set aside.
5. Heat the ghee/oil in a thick bottomed oven proof dish and add the meat mixture, fry for a minute. Then add rice over it and drizzle a little ghee/oil and saffron milk. Add the remaining onions, coriander, mint leaves.
6. Cover the dish with foil and cover with a heavy lid. Cook in the oven gas mark 7 / 220°C for 30-40 minutes.

Wedding Style Black Chickpeas
(Tingy Tangy)

This dish always reminds me of the food served at Indian weddings. It was a favourite and we used to always go back for seconds. When I tried to recreate it with my mum she had to think back to the times when she cooked the wedding food with her elders. This is our version of that dish, which we have nicknamed 'Tingy Tangy Chickpea'.

INGREDIENTS

- **800g black chickpeas in water (drain and rinse)**
- **3 tbsp gram flour**
- **2 tbsp sunflower oil**
- **1 tsp mustard seeds**
- **400g chopped tomatoes**
- **2 tsp salt (to taste)**
- **1 ½ tsp coriander & cumin powder**
- **¾ tsp garam masala**
- **½ tsp turmeric powder**
- **½ tsp red chilli powder**
- **1 tsp crushed garlic**
- **1 tsp chopped ginger**
- **2 tbsp jaggery (to taste)**
- **2 tbsp tomato ketchup**
- **handful fresh coriander chopped**

SERVES	SPICE	DIFFICULTY
6		

HOW TO COOK

1. Place the oil in a cooking pan and heat, add the mustard seeds and wait until they pop and then add the gram flour and cook until light brown.
2. Add the tomatoes, stir and cook on a medium heat.
3. Add all the spices including salt, garlic, ginger and cook for 10 minutes on a medium to low heat.
4. Pour some hot water into the pan if the sauce is too thick and gradually stir.
5. Add the black chickpeas, jaggery and ketchup and cook further for 5 minutes.
6. Add water as required. Taste and add more salt or jaggery to your tastes.
7. Add the fresh coriander, serve with cumin rice or chapattis.

WADOO
(SPROUTED BEANS)

Mung beans sprouted and cooked with other lentils. I used to have to wash up and serve this on a special day in the Indian calendar when the mums were fasting. Positive thing was I got paid to do it. Generally served with rotla's, Indian bread made out of juwar flour.

INGREDIENTS

- **700g sprouted mung beans, or mixed sprouted beans.**
- **4 tbsp sunflower oil**
- **½ tsp mustard seeds**
- **1 tsp salt (to taste)**
- **2 tsp coriander & cumin powder**
- **1 tsp garam masala**
- **½ tsp turmeric powder**
- **½ tsp red chilli powder**
- **1 ½ tsp crushed garlic**
- **1 tsp chopped ginger**
- **2 tsp chopped green chillies**
- **2 tsp lemon juice**
- **handful fresh coriander chopped**

MAKES	SPICE	DIFFICULTY
4		

HOW TO COOK

1. Place the oil in a cooking pan and heat, add mustard seeds and wait until they sizzle/pop.
2. Add the sprouted beans and stir.
3. Add all the other ingredients except the coriander and stir.
4. Cook on low heat with the lid on for 30-40 minutes until the beans can be squashed. Stir from time to time.
5. If it starts to stick add a little hot water.
6. Add the coriander and serve with chapattis or use as a filling for wraps.

SHRIKHAND

A popular dish sometimes served at weddings or events leading up to the big occasion. Our version of ice cream, great on its own or served with fruit.

INGREDIENTS

- **200g curd cheese or cream cheese**
- **icing sugar (to taste)**
- **1 tsp crushed green cardamon seeds**
- **pinch saffron**
- **flaked almonds**

HOW TO COOK

1. Mix the sugar and curd cheese until dissolved and light and smooth. Add more icing sugar to your level of sweetness.
2. In a small bowl add the saffron and 1 tbsp warm water. Then add to the cream and mix.
3. Stir in the ground cardamon and flaked almonds.
4. Serve over any fruit but equally nice on its own.

NOTE: If you want a more runny texture then add some double cream or use greek yoghurt.

SERVES 4

DIFFICULTY

Coconut Ice-Cream

I often get asked to make this for my girly get together. I love coconut and in an ice cream you can't go wrong.

INGREDIENTS

- **350ml full fat milk**
- **75g desiccated coconut**
- **350ml single cream**
- **2 medium eggs**
- **2 medium egg yolks**
- **100g sugar**
- **¼ tsp salt**

SERVES 4

DIFFICULTY

HOW TO COOK

1. Scald the milk, coconut and cream in a pan over a low heat for 15-20 minutes.
2. Push through a fine sieve, pressing out as much of the coconut juice as possible, (if you like the texture add a bit of the coconut back in the mixture).
3. Beat the eggs and egg yolks, sugar and salt with an electric whisk until thick and mousse-like.
4. Place over a pan of simmering water, stir in some of the coconut cream mixture, then the remainder and cook until the mixture will coat the back of a spoon.
5. Cool quickly, then pour into freezer trays and freeze until mushy. Beat again to break up the ice crystals, return to the freezer.
6. Freeze until firm, about 2-3 hours.
7. Before serving, remove from freezer for 30 minutes, scoop into chilled glasses.

MANGO & PISTACHIO CHEESECAKE

One of my signature dishes. Baked cheesecake with mango and a base using pistachios. It needs to be done a day in advance but well worth the effort.

INGREDIENTS

FOR THE PISTACHIO BASE:

- **470g shelled raw unsalted pistachio nuts**
- **60g granulated sugar**
- **¼ teaspoon sea salt**
- **4 tablespoons unsalted butter (melted)**

FOR THE MANGO CHEESE FILLING:

- **450g cream cheese (room temperature)**
- **240g white granulated sugar**
- **2 eggs (room temperature)**
- **2 egg yolks (room temperature)**
- **250g mango pulp**
- **1 teaspoon green cardamon seeds (ground)**

MAKES SPICE DIFFICULTY

12 SLICES

HOW TO PREPARE

1. First, make the pistachio crust: position one rack in the lowest position and another in the centre of the oven, preheat the oven to gas mark 5 / 190°C. Lightly butter the bottom and sides of a 9 inch spring form pan.

2. Put the pistachios in a food processes and pulse until they are ground to the consistency of fine breadcrumbs, (if the pieces are too large, you will have a problem making them stick together when you pat the crust into the pan). Transfer the ground nuts to a medium sized bowl, and stir in the sugar and salt.

3. Pour the melted butter into the mixture and use your hand to thoroughly combine the ingredients. The mixture should have the texture of slightly coarse wet sand. With your finger tips spread out the mixture evenly across the bottom, make sure the bottom is completely covered so the filling doesn't leak through while it is baking.

4. Place the pan on the centre rack of the oven and bake until the crust is golden brown, 10-12 minutes. Remove the pan from the oven and set aside to cool. Reduce the oven temperature to gas mark 3 / 170°C.

5. Before you start the filling make sure the cream cheese is completely softened and the eggs are at room temperature.

6. Place the cream cheese in a mixer bowl. When the mixer is on medium speed, beat it, adding the sugar, ¼ cup at a time, and beating until the mixture is smooth and creamy. Occasionally stop the mixer and scrape the sides of the bowl with a spatula. Don't worry about over beating.

Continued on page 114.

INGREDIENTS

FOR THE PISTACHIO BASE:

- **470g shelled raw unsalted pistachio nuts**
- **60g granulated sugar**
- **¼ teaspoon sea salt**
- **4 tablespoons unsalted butter (melted)**

FOR THE MANGO CHEESE FILLING:

- **450g cream cheese (room temperature)**
- **240g white granulated sugar**
- **2 eggs (room temperature)**
- **2 egg yolks (room temperature)**
- **250g mango pulp**
- **1 teaspoon green cardamon seeds (ground)**

MAKES	SPICE	DIFFICULTY
12 SLICES		

Continued from page 112.

7. Turn the mixer off, add 1 egg, and then beat on low speed until the egg has blended with the cheese. Turn off the mixer, add the second egg and then repeat. Do the same with the 2 egg yolks, adding them one at a time. Please be careful because overbeating the egg can make deep cracks in the cheesecake.

8. Scrape all the batter off the paddle or whips and add it to the bowl. Pour the mango pulp into the bowl; sprinkle the ground cardamon evenly over it. Stir until the pulp blends into the batter. Pour the batter into the baked crust.

9. Fill a shallow pan with boiling water and place on the lower oven rack. This will provide steam, which is essential as it will ensure a creamy filling and an unburnt crust. Place the spring form pan on the center oven rack, then bake for 30 minutes.

10. Reduce the oven temperature to gas mark 2 / 160°C and continue to bake the cheesecake until the center jiggles when slightly nudged, 20-30 minutes.

11. Carefully remove the pan from the oven and set it on a cooling rack. Let the cheesecake cool completely at room temperature before you refrigerate it, (this will stop the cheesecake from splitting.)

12. Refrigerate the cheesecake, uncovered, for at least 12 hours and no more then 24 hours before serving it.

SERVING TIP: When you're cutting the cheesecake run a sharp knife round the sides to loosen the cheesecake. Open and remove the springform sides, cut into quarters and then individual slices ensuring you wipe clean the knife after each cut.

GULAB JAMUN

I didn't really like this dessert as it was too sweet until I came across those made by my mother-in-law. This is her recipe and she makes great ones that all the family enjoy, not too sweet but just right. You can freeze them as well so don't think you need to eat them all, but then I wouldn't blame you.

INGREDIENTS

JAMUNS:

- **450g fine milk powder**
- **115g plain flour**
- **1 tsp ENO (or bicarbonate of soda)**
- **1 ½ tsp crushed green cardamon seeds**
- **230ml water**
- **75ml milk**
- **sunflower oil for deep frying**

SYRUP:

- **350g sugar**
- **800ml water**

MAKES **50** | SPICE | DIFFICULTY

HOW TO PREPARE

1. Make the syrup first. In a large saucepan heat the sugar with the water until dissolved. Cook for 15-20 minutes until it thickens to create a syrup. Cool on one side.
2. Mix the dry ingredients, then add the water and milk to create a crumble texture. Then bind into a soft dough.
3. Heat the oil in a deep fry pan. When ready, create small balls with the dough and add to the oil, a few at a time as the dough balls double in size.
4. Fry on a low heat and rotate as they fry until medium brown colour (about 3-4 minutes).
5. Remove and cool.
6. Add the balls to the syrup and serve with a little of the syrup.

Breads & Rice

Staples to have with your meal or on their own.

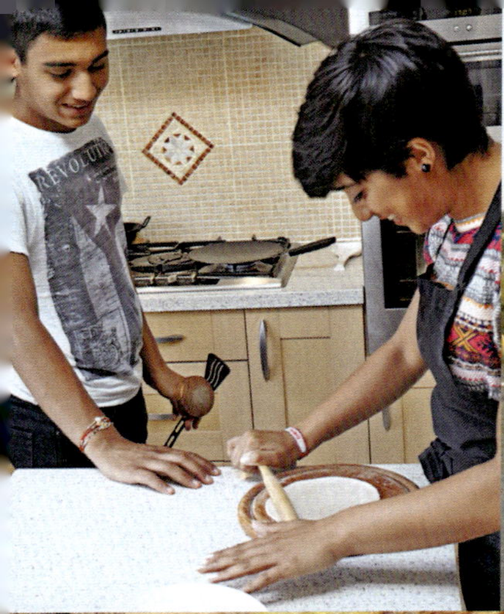

CHAPATTIS

Indian flatbread eaten most days and enjoyed by all, especially the children smothered with butter.

INGREDIENTS

- **400g chapatti flour**
- **3 tbsp sunflower oil**
- **300ml hot water**

SERVES 4

DIFFICULTY

HOW TO MAKE THE DOUGH

1. In a bowl, add the flour and oil and rub together.
2. Gradually add the hot water to form pliable dough, soft enough to roll.
3. Break the dough up into small balls (fist full, 20)
4. Place chapatti pan or frying pan onto a medium heat.
5. Flour surface and roll out dough into a circle, approximately 14-16cm in diameter, (size of a side plate).
6. Place into the pan, cook on one side, see bubbles appear underneath. Turn over.
7. Turn over again and gently aid the bread to rise by pressing with the chapatti maker (30 seconds to a minute).
8. Take off the heat and place on a side plate. Butter if required.
9. Serve with any main meal.

Poori

*Deep friend bread made similar to chapatti
but fried and the size of a saucer.*

INGREDIENTS

- **200g chapatti flour**
- **1 ½ tbsp sunflower oil**
- **½ tsp salt**
- **125ml warm to hot water**
- **sunflower oil for frying**

HOW TO COOK

1. In a bowl, add the flour and oil and rub together.
2. Gradually add the water to form a firm but pliable dough.
3. Break the dough up into small balls .
4. Add the oil to a wok or deep frying pan and heat.
5. Roll out each dough ball into a circle, approximately 7cm diameter.
6. Fry each poori, gently pat with a slotted spoon, to encourage it to puff up. Turn and cook on the other side, (take approximately 1 minute per poori).
7. Drain on kitchen paper.
8. Serve with any main meal.

MAKES **20**

DIFFICULTY

Methi Paratha

Flavoured chapatti with a crispy edge to them. These are great as accompaniments or for breakfast.

INGREDIENTS

- **400g chapatti flour**
- **3 tbsp sunflower oil**
- **300ml hot water**
- **2 tsp ground cumin powder**
- **1 tsp red chilli powder**
- **½ tsp turmeric powder**
- **½ tsp salt (to taste)**
- **½ bunch of fresh methi leaves (fenugreek)**
- **2 tbsp sesame seeds (optional)**
- **butter/oil for frying**

MAKES	SPICE	DIFFICULTY
15		

HOW TO MAKE THE DOUGH

1. In a bowl, add the flour and oil and rub together. Add all the other dry ingredients.
2. Gradually add the hot water to form a pliable dough, soft enough to roll.

HOW TO COOK

3. Break the dough up into 15 medium sized balls.
4. Place a chapatti pan or frying pan onto a medium heat.
5. Flour surface and roll the dough out into a circle, about 14cm in diameter, (size of a side plate).
6. Place into the pan, cook on one side until you see bubbles appear underneath. Turn over, and cook on this side for 30 seconds. Spread some butter/oil mixture on the top.
7. Turn over again and cook for a minute. Spread the butter/oil on the other side, turn and cook for 1 minute.
8. Take off the heat and place on a side plate. Repeat this process until all are rolled out and cooked.
9. Serve with any main meal, on their own for breakfast or as a wrap.

Bhatura

Punjabi style bread that is a cross between a naan bread and a chapatti.

INGREDIENTS

- **450g self raising flour**
- **255g plain yoghurt**
- **1 tbsp of cumin seeds roasted and lightly crushed**
- **1 tbsp dried fenugreek leaves (optional)**
- **2 tsp oil**
- **1 tsp salt**
- **water to combine into dough**
- **sunflower oil for deep frying**

MAKES 20 | SPICE | DIFFICULTY

HOW TO COOK

1. Combine the yoghurt, cumin seeds, flour, salt and oil into a bowl and blend the ingredients together with your fingers. Add the water to form a rough dough.
2. Add a little oil to your hands and knead to form a smooth dough.
3. Cover with a cloth and let it sit for 5-6 hrs.
4. Divide into small balls (about 20) and roll out into 10cm discs.
5. Put some oil enough for deep frying into a pan and heat.
6. Fry in hot oil (180-190˚C), one or two a time for 1-2 minutes. Gently pat with a slotted spoon, to encourage it to puff up. Turn and cook on the other side.
7. Drain on kitchen paper and repeat.
8. Serve as an accompaniment with any Indian main meal.

Boiled Basmati Rice

Classic way to cook perfect rice.

INGREDIENTS

- **basmati rice (handful per individual)**
- **salt to taste**
- **hot water**

DIFFICULTY

HOW TO COOK

1. Wash and soak the rice for 30 minutes.
2. Boil water in a kettle and then add to the pan.
3. Place the rice into the hot water, add the salt and boil on a medium heat.
4. Do not let the water disappear. The rice will be cooked once you can squeeze the grains.
5. Drain and then place in a microwavable dish/bowl.
6. Microwave for 2 minutes, just before eating. Add butter if desired.

NOTE: Why not add a few cloves and stick cinnamon to flavour the rice as it boils.

Cumin & Saffron Rice

This combination came from a demonstration I performed at a local food and drink show and has become a family favourite.

INGREDIENTS

- **150g basmati rice**
- **1 tsp cumin seeds**
- **2 tbsp sunflower oil**
- **pinch saffron**
- **350ml hot water**

HOW TO COOK

1. Wash and soak the rice for 30 minutes. Put the saffron and 1 tbsp warm water in a small bowl and set to one side.
2. Drain the rice and put to one side. Add the oil to a pan and heat. Add the cumin seeds and wait until they turn brown.
3. Add rice into the oil and stir slowly for 1-2 minutes.
4. Add the hot water and saffron to the pan. Stir gently.
5. Turn the heat down to medium/low and cover. Cook until the water has all evaporated and the rice is cooked (approximately 8 minutes).
6. Serve as an accompaniment to any Indian main dish.

SERVES	SPICE	DIFFICULTY
4		

Lemon Rice

Curry leaves and lemon give this rice its essential flavour.
Often created when using up left over rice.

INGREDIENTS

- **450g cooked basmati rice**
- **1 tsp cumin seeds**
- **4 curry leaves**
- **½ tsp red chilli powder**
- **½ tsp turmeric powder**
- **1 tsp salt (to taste)**
- **1 tsp chopped green chillies**
- **1 tsp sugar**
- **2 tbsp lemon juice**
- **3 tbsp sunflower oil**
- **handful fresh coriander chopped**

SERVES	SPICE	DIFFICULTY
4		

HOW TO COOK

1. In a mixing bowl add the rice, ground spices, salt, sugar, lemon juice and coriander. Mix and put to one side.
2. In a frying pan heat the oil and then add the cumin seeds and curry leaves and cook for 30 seconds.
3. Add the rice and stir. Pan should be on a medium to low heat.
4. Cook for 5 minutes stirring slowly. Ensure the rice has heated through.
5. Serve hot with any main dish.

Kashmir Saffron Rice

Rich and aromoatic pilau rice, with stronger spices, raisins and nuts.

INGREDIENTS

- 200g basmati rice (washed and soaked)
- 4 tbsp sunflower oil
- ½ tsp cumin seeds
- 7½ cm cinnamon stick
- 3 cloves
- 3 green cardamon pods
- 1 bay leaf
- 1 small onion (sliced)
- 20g raisins
- pinch of saffron (soaked in 2 tbsp warm milk)
- 1 tsp salt
- lots of freshly ground black pepper (to taste)
- 15g pistachios

SERVES **6** SPICE DIFFICULTY

HOW TO COOK

1. Heat the oil in a saucepan. Add the whole spices and bay leaf and wait until they sizzle. Add the onion and cook until soft and golden, then add the raisins and cook for a couple of minutes.
2. Add the drained rice to the pan. Stir into the spiced oil and then add 400ml of water, the saffron milk and salt.
3. Bring to the boil for a couple of minutes, then reduce the heat(low), cover and cook for 7-8 minutes. Taste and test the grains are cooked otherwise leave for another minute or so.
4. Add the pistachios and black pepper and fluff up with a fork as you stir them in. Leave to rest for 4 minutes. This allows any excess water to evaporate.
5. Serve hot with any main dish or on its own.

Samosa Pastry

Alternative buttery pastry for your samosa's.

INGREDIENTS

- **250g plain flour**
- **60g butter**
- **75ml warm milk**

MAKES | SPICE | DIFFICULTY

12

HOW TO COOK

1. Add the flour and butter and rub together.
2. Gradually add the warm milk to form a pliable dough, soft enough to roll.

See Vegetable Samosa recipe (page 90).

Preserves & Dips

A selection of some old and new recipes. Great as an accompaniment to a meal or with salad and poppadoms

Coriander, Tomato & Chilli Dip

INGREDIENTS

- 3 tbsp finely chopped coriander
- 1 chopped green chillies
- 1 tsp chopped ginger
- ¼ tsp salt
- 2 fresh tomatoes (skinned)
- ¼ tsp sugar

SPICE DIFFICULTY

HOW TO PREPARE

1. Mix all the ingredients together in a bowl. Process in a blender or in a pestle and mortar.
2. Can be served with lamb chops or any Indian starter.

Tamarind Dip

INGREDIENTS

- 100g block of tamarind
- 2 tsp chopped green chillies
- 1 tbsp fresh coriander chopped
- 2 tbsp grated jaggery
- salt to season
- hot water

SPICE DIFFICULTY

HOW TO PREPARE

1. Tamarind pulp needs to be soaked in hot water before use. Break up the pulp and soak for about 20 minutes to soften.
2. Strain through a sieve into a bowl, pressing to extract as much flavour as possible.
3. Melt the jaggery with a little water and add to the tamarind
4. Mix all the ingredients together in a bowl.

Raita

INGREDIENTS

- 225g natural yoghurt
- ½ cucumber (grated)
- 1 tsp mustard seeds crushed
- pinch salt, red chilli and turmeric powder
- ½ tsp sugar

SPICE DIFFICULTY

HOW TO PREPARE

1. Squeeze the water out of the grated cucumber and add to the yoghurt.
2. Add all the other ingredients and mix well.
3. Serve with any main or starter dish

Hot Pineapple Chutney

INGREDIENTS

- 1kg pineapple chunks
- 200ml water
- 11g garlic puree
- 5g ginger puree
- 700g sugar
- 5g chilli powder
- 150 ml white wine vinegar
- 5g crushed red chilli flakes
- 3 cloves whole
- 4g green cardamon powder
- 5g coriander & cumin powder
- ¼ tsp onion seeds
- ½ tsp salt
- ½ tsp mustard seeds
- ½ tsp cumin seeds

SPICE DIFFICULTY

HOW TO COOK

1. In a large saucepan or wide based preserving pan, add the vinegar, garlic, ginger all the spices and bring to a boil.
2. Simmer gently for 5 minutes to create a spiced vinegar.
3. Add the sugar, water and stir until the sugar has dissolved to create a syrup.
4. Add in the pineapple chunks. Turn the heat down to a slow cook and allow to cook and thicken.
5. The chutney will be ready when you can place a spoon at the bottom of the pan and drag the mixture to form a tram line that comes back together slowly.
6. Spoon hot into clean jars and lid. Leave for a couple of weeks before using.

Grated Apple Chutney

INGREDIENTS

- 300g cooking apples (grated)
- 2 tsp salt
- 3 tsp granulated sugar
- 140g granulated sugar
- ¾ tsp red chilli powder
- ½ tsp turmeric powder
- 5cm stick cinnamon
- 5 cloves
- ½ tsp mustard seeds

MAKES SPICE DIFFICULTY

2 JARS

HOW TO COOK

1. Skin and grate each cooking apple and put on a tray. Sprinkle half the salt and 3 tsp of granulated sugar over the apple, leave overnight or alternatively leave for at least 2 hrs. This will release the water from the apples.
2. Next squeeze the grated apple to remove the water and put in a bowl.
3. In a saucepan, add the oil and heat.
4. Once the oil is warm add the cinnamon, cloves and mustard seeds and wait until they pop.
5. Add the apple and cook on a low heat. Mix in the remaining salt, sugar and stir. Then add the powdered spices and cook until the apples are soft and the sugar carmalises until the chutney thickens.
6. Bottle the chutney into jars and keep in the fridge.

NOTE: Great with cheese or as an accompaniment to a vegetarian meal.

Tomato & Onion Relish

INGREDIENTS

- **600g chopped plum tomatoes**
- **200g onions, finely chopped**
- **32ml sunflower oil**
- **¼ tsp onion seeds**
- **¾ tsp fennel seeds**
- **¾ tsp mustard seeds**
- **¾ tsp cumin seeds**
- **¼ tsp red chilli powder**
- **250g sugar**
- **150ml distilled malt vinegar**
- **½ tsp salt**
- **¼ tsp black pepper**

MAKES SPICE DIFFICULTY

3/4
8OZ JARS

HOW TO COOK

1. Take a large saucepan or wide based preserving pan. Add the oil and heat.
2. Add the following whole spices, onion seeds, fennel, mustard and cumin seeds.
3. Once they sizzle and pop, add the onions and tomatoes and cook for a couple of minutes.
4. Then add the other ingredients.
5. Cook on a medium heat, stirring occasionally until the tomatoes start to break down and onions soften.
6. Check for seasoning and continue to cook until the chutney thickens.
7. Chutney is ready when you can drag a spoon at the bottom of the pan and it takes a few seconds for chutney to come back together. You would expect the volume to be reduced to half.
8. Bottle into clean jars and lid.
9. Should last a year sealed in a jar, once opened refrigerate and use within 4 weeks.

Kickin' Coriander Dressing

INGREDIENTS

- 200ml olive oil
- 90ml white wine vinegar
- 90ml water
- 6g garlic powder
- 5g chaat masala
- 3.5g salt
- 3.5g red chilli powder
- 15g coriander & cumin powder
- 6g dry coriander leaves

SPICE DIFFICULTY

HOW TO PREPARE

1. Mix all the ingredients together with a blender.
2. Store in a jar or bottle.
3. Drizzle over salads or use as a marinade over chicken or fish.

Marvellous Mango Dressing

INGREDIENTS

- 170ml mango pulp
- 100ml olive oil
- 3.5g red chilli powder
- 3.5g cumin seeds
- 100ml white wine vinegar

SPICE DIFFICULTY

HOW TO PREPARE

1. Mix all the ingredients together with a blender.
2. Store in a jar or bottle.
3. Drizzle over salads.

Index

// Acknowledgments

Thank you to my mum, Pushpaben, for her patience in teaching me her recipes and helping me put together some of the old traditions on paper in order for us to keep the legacy of our food for future generations. My dad to whom I often cooked treats and he gladly ate them.

My mother-in-law, Kundanben, for the Gulab Jamun recipes and more, showing me a different style of cooking to my own mum.

I would also like to thank my photographer, Sue Hiscoe, for pushing me to do the book and for her advice throughout. Also thanks for the great photos, styling and tea during the sessions. Our days cooking and shooting will always be remembered, especially the rainy days in Halifax under the extreme conditions of the production unit.

My three children, who have been very involved in helping me whether it was in preparing the ingredients, eating the food or getting involved in the photography. However, most of all, for being very excited about the book.

Thank you to Elaine Lemm, friend and food and drink writer, for editing and advice on my book given her own pressures of work.

Also I would like to thank my colleague, Alison, for checking the recipes and often testing them for me. My friends for proof reading the book in such short timescales.

Most of all to my husband, Paresh, for his support, encouragement and belief in me throughout this process, and putting up with my stress levels!

From the Children

ROWAN (AGE 15)

"As a teenage boy the most important thing is to ensure that my stomach is full with healthy yet tasty food. Thanks to mum the food is always delicious and this book will allow me to replicate my favourites, such as lamb curry or fish masala when I get older."

NIRAN (AGE 10)

"We normally cook as a family and mum's the head chef! The food is nice and I hope you enjoy it."

NAYESHA (AGE 17)

"Since we were young, we have all helped out in the kitchen, whether it was helping to cook a chicken curry or rolling out chapattis. I can remember mum helping us cut out teletubby shaped chapattis and cooking them for us to eat. Family and eating together has always been important to us; something I would like to carry through in to my future family. I am very excited by the book and it will be very useful when I am at university."

"Eating the variety of dishes mum cooked during the production of the book, especially those we only ate on special occasions, is always a reason to love mum and her business."

Nayesha (age 17)

Prett's 'Family Secrets' reflects a lifetime's worth of knowledge inspired by the influence of previous generations.

NIGEL BARDEN